THIS IS OUR FAITH

Series Authors: Janaan Manternach
Carl J. Pfeifer

Authors: Jo'Ann Chiarani
Joan R. DeMerchant
Maureen Gallagher
Jean Marie Weber

Contributing authors: Sister Carolyn Puccio, C.S.J.
Kate Sweeney Ristow

SILVER BURDETT GINN
PARSIPPANY, NJ

THIS IS OUR FAITH
SCHOOL PROGRAM

Contributing authors: James Bitney, Sister Cecilia Maureen Cromwell, I.H.M., Patricia Frevert, Robert M. Hamma, Mary Lou Ihrig, Paula A. Lenz, Judene Leon, Yvette Nelson, Sister Arlene Pomije, C.S.J., Sister Carolyn Puccio, C.S.J., Anna Ready, Kate Sweeney Ristow, Sister Mary Agnes Ryan, I.H.M., Sister Maureen Shaughnessy, S.C., Brother Michael Sheerin, F.M.S., Barbara Carol Vasiloff

Opening Doors: A Take-Home Magazine: Peter H.M. Demkovitz, Janie Gustafson, Margaret Savitskas

Day to Day: Skills for Christian Living: Susan G. Keys

Advisory Board:

Rev. Louis J. Cameli

Philip J. Cunningham

Sister Clare E. Fitzgerald

William J. Freburger

Greer G. Gordon

Sister Veronica R. Grover, S.H.C.J.

Rev. Thomas Guarino

Rev. Robert E. Harahan

Kathleen Hendricks

Rev. Eugene LaVerdieré, S.S.S.

Rev. Frank J. McNulty

Rev. Msgr. John J. Strynkowski

Consultants: Linda Blanchette, Anita Bridge, Fred Brown, Rod Brownfield, Sister Mary Michael Burns, S.C., Patricia Burns, Bernadine Carroll, Mary Ellen Cocks, Sister Peggy Conlon, R.S.M., Mary Ann Crowley, Pamela Danni, Sister Jamesetta DeFelice, O.S.U., Sister Mary Elizabeth Duke, S.N.D., Mary M. Gibbons, Yolando Gremillion, Sister Angela Hallahan, C.H.F., Alice J. Heard, Sister Michele O'Connoll, P.B.V.M., Sister Angela O'Mahoney, P.B.V.M., Sister Ruthann O'Mara, S.S.J., Sandra Okulicz-Hulme, Judy Papandria, Rachel Pasano, Sallie Ann Phelan, Sister Geraldine M. Rogers, S.S.J., Mary Lou Schlosser, Patricia Ann Sibilia, Margaret E. Skelly, Lisa Ann Sorlie, Sister Victorine Stoltz, O.S.B., Sister Nancy Jean Turner, S.H.C.J., Christine Ward, Judith Reidel Weber, Kay White, Elizabeth M. Williams, Catherine R. Wolf, Florence Bambrick Yarney, Kathryn K. Zapcic

Nihil Obstat

Kathleen Flanagan, S.C., Ph.D.
Censor Librorum

Ellen Joyce, S.C., Ph.D.
Censor Librorum

Imprimatur

✠ Most Rev. Frank J. Rodimer
   Bishop of Paterson

November 22, 1996

The *nihil obstat* and *imprimatur* are official declarations that a book or pamphlet is free of doctrinal and moral error. No implication is contained therein that those who have granted the *nihil obstat* and *imprimatur* agree with the contents, opinions, or statements expressed.

ACKNOWLEDGMENTS

Excerpts from *The New American Bible* © 1970 by the Confraternity of Christian Doctrine are used by permission of the copyright owner.

Excerpts from *The New American Bible with Revised New Testament* © 1986, 1970 by the Confraternity of Christian Doctrine, Washington, D.C. 20017. Used with permission. All rights reserved.

All adaptations of Scripture are based on *The New American Bible with Revised New Testament*.

Excerpts from the English translation of *Rite of Baptism for Children* © 1969, International Committee on English in the Liturgy, Inc. (ICEL); the English translation of psalm responses from the *Lectionary for Mass* © 1969, ICEL; excerpts from the English translation of *The Roman Missal* © 1973, ICEL; excerpts from the English translation of *Rite of Penance* © 1974, ICEL; excerpts from the English translation of *Rite of Confirmation*, Second Edition © 1975, ICEL; excerpts from the English translation of *Pastoral Care of the Sick: Rites of Anointing and Viaticum* © 1982, ICEL. All rights reserved.

Excerpt from the *Lectionary for Masses with Children* Copyright ©1991, United States Catholic Conference, Washington, D.C. Used with permission.

Excerpts from an article by Sr. Thea Bowman, F.S.P.A. in *Lead Me, Guide Me: The African American Catholic Hymnal* published by G.I.A. Publications, Inc. are reprinted by permission.

ISBN 0–382–30496–9

Contents ～～～～～～～

Let Us Pray

The Lord's Prayer

Our Father, who art in heaven,
   hallowed be thy name;
thy kingdom come;
thy will be done on earth
   as it is in heaven.
Give us this day our daily bread;
and forgive us our trespasses
   as we forgive those
   who trespass against us;
and lead us not into temptation,
   but deliver us from evil.
Amen.

Padre Nuestro

Padre nuestro, que estás en el cielo,
   santificado sea tu nombre;
venga a nosotros tu reino;
hágase tu voluntad en la tierra
   como en el cielo.
Danos hoy nuestro pan de cada día;
perdona nuestras ofensas,
   como también nosotros
      perdonamos
   a los que nos ofenden;
no nos dejes caer en la tentación,
   y líbranos del mal.
Amén.

Sign of the Cross

In the name of the Father,
   and of the Son,
   and of the Holy Spirit.
Amen.

Señal de la Cruz

En el nombre del Padre
   y del Hijo
   y del Espíritu Santo.
Amén.

Hail Mary

Hail Mary, full of grace,
the Lord is with you.
Blessed are you among women,
and blessed is the fruit
of your womb, Jesus.
Holy Mary, Mother of God,
pray for us sinners, now,
and at the hour of our death.
Amen.

Ave María

Dios te salve, María, llena eres
de gracia,
el Señor es contigo.
Bendita tú eres entre todas las
mujeres,
y bendito es el fruto
de tu vientre, Jesús.
Santa María, Madre de Dios,
ruega por nosotros, pecadores,
ahora y en la hora de nuestra
muerte.
Amén.

Glory Be to the Father

Glory be to the Father,
and to the Son,
and to the Holy Spirit.
As it was in the beginning,
is now, and ever shall be,
world without end.
Amen.

Gloria al Padre

Gloria al Padre,
y al Hijo,
y al Espíritu Santo.
Como era en el principio,
ahora y siempre,
por los siglos de los siglos.
Amén.

Let Us Pray

Morning Prayer

My God, I offer you today,
    all that I think and do and say,
    and ask for your blessing
    as you lead me in your ways.
Amen.

Evening Prayer

My God, before I sleep tonight
    I want to thank you
    for being with me today.
As I close my eyes to rest,
    keep me in your loving care.
Amen.

Grace Before Meals

Bless us, O Lord,
    and these your gifts,
    which we are about to receive
    from your goodness,
    through Christ our Lord.
Amen.

Grace After Meals

We give thanks, O God,
    for these and all your gifts,
    which we have received
    through Christ our Lord.
Amen.

Prayer of Sorrow

My God,
I am sorry for my sins with all my heart.
In choosing to do wrong
and failing to do good,
I have sinned against you
whom I should love above all things.
I firmly intend, with your help,
to do penance,
to sin no more,
and to avoid whatever leads me to sin.

Revised Rite of Penance

Apostles' Creed

I believe in God, the Father almighty,
    creator of heaven and earth.

I believe in Jesus Christ, his only Son, our Lord.
    He was conceived by the power of the Holy Spirit
        and born of the Virgin Mary.
    He suffered under Pontius Pilate,
        was crucified, died, and was buried.
    He descended to the dead.
    On the third day he rose again.
    He ascended into heaven,
        and is seated at the right hand of the Father.
    He will come again to judge the living and the dead.

I believe in the Holy Spirit,
    the holy catholic Church,
    the communion of saints,
    the forgiveness of sins,
    the resurrection of the body
    and life everlasting. Amen.

Let Us Pray

Prayer to the Holy Spirit

Come, Holy Spirit,
 fill the hearts of your faithful,
 and kindle in them
 the fire of your love.
Send forth your Spirit, O Lord,
 and they shall be created.
And you shall renew
 the face of the earth.
Amen.

Beginning the Journey

We are growing up as God's children. We meet new people in God's family. We learn about new places.

Here are some things I would like to do with my class this year.

_____

_____

Here are my drawings of some of God's special people and places that I like best. As I begin my third-grade journey, I remember what these people and places mean to me.

Here are some things about Jesus and the Church that I want to find out about this year.

_____

_____

Each time we meet together this year, we will learn more about what it means to be members of the Catholic Church.

Prayer for the Journey

Leader: As members of the Church, we are on a special journey. Jesus is our leader. The Holy Spirit is our helper and guide. Friends and followers of Jesus all over the world are traveling with us on our journey. Will you join me on this special journey?

All: We will.

Leader: As a sign of our commitment—our promise—to journey together, let us sign our names on the covenant inside the front cover of our books. Now let's read together what we will do on our journey as Christians.

Leader: Almost since the beginning, Jesus' followers have had a special way of saying what they believe as Christians. We call this our creed. Our parents and friends said a creed for us at our Baptism. We can say a creed together now. We will learn more about what our creed means as we journey through this year together.

All: *This is our faith. This is the faith of the Church. We are proud to profess our faith in Christ Jesus our Lord. Amen.*

- based on the bishop's proclamation in the *Rite of Confirmation*

8

THIS IS OUR FAITH

SILVER BURDETT GINN • SCHOOL PROGRAM

3

A Preview of Grade **3**

OPENING DOORS
A Take-Home Magazine ™

We hope you will join us . . . .

A Profile of the Third-Grade Child

As parent or guardian, you will want to relate to your maturing third grader in the most effective way possible. As an eight-year-old child begins moving toward independence, he or she needs the love, approval, guidance, and reinforcement of a supportive family. Your child is changing in many ways.

- Curious about life, nature, and people, many third graders prefer to learn from their own observations.

- Mastering the ability to read and to reason, they can be more exciting and challenging to teach.

- An increased social sense places great emphasis on friendships and increases a third grader's willingness to share. It also makes them more self-conscious about being criticized in front of their friends.

Third graders learn best when they

- have guidelines and rules to follow.
- are assigned simple tasks that allow for success and build self-esteem.
- can trust significant adults who care for them.
- know that their feelings are accepted.

Taking Time Take the time this week to talk to your third grader about his or her daily responsibilities at home and at school. Be sure that your expectations are reasonable. Express to your child the confidence you have that he or she can meet those expectations.

This Year in Grade 3

The focus of Grade 3 is the Church and the kind of community the Church is called to be. The mission, the message, the prayer, and the actions of God's special family will be explored.

In Unit 1 your child will learn about the community of Jesus'

friends and will consider some of the joys and challenges of living as one, holy, catholic, and apostolic Church. Your third grader will look at these priorities of the early Christian communities and will come to understand how they continue to guide the people of God today.

for an adventure that will give you and your third grader a closer look at the life of the Church. As your child promises, in faith, to seek a greater understanding of the Church this year, you are invited aboard as the most important guide in your child's faith life and as a cojourneyer who learns alongside of your young companion.

OPENING DOORS
A Take-Home Magazine™

OPENING DOORS is a take-home magazine you can look forward to receiving each time your child completes a unit of THIS IS OUR FAITH. It is our hope that the features of each magazine will help to open the doors of faith- and story-sharing in your home as you and your child grow together in faith.

A Closer Look

includes an adult-level reflection on the theme of the unit with a focus on the Mass and family pages for you to enjoy with your child.

Being Catholic

highlights something special about our American Catholic heritage.

Growing Closer

suggests activities to help you and your family integrate your faith into everyday life.

And also...

Looking Ahead

previews the next unit of THIS IS OUR FAITH.

UNIT 1

A Marked Community

Why would you want to belong to a group like this?

Our Church Is One

Surprising Teamwork

The Bobcats' record was not very good—four losses, one tie, no wins. Before the final quarter of the game against the Raiders began, Pam, the Bobcats' coach, called them together.

"Why do you think you're not winning?" Pam asked in a kind but firm voice.

"They're better than we are," Laura said sadly.

"They are not," Jillian argued. "It's because we're all ball hoggers."

"I think you're right," Pam agreed. "So let's go back in there and play like a team! Pass the ball and talk to each other. You can only win by playing *together*."

Then, for the first time all season, it happened. The Bobcats started working together. They talked out loud to one another, "I've got it!" "You take it, Andra!" "Over here!" "Pass it to Laura!" "Keep going!" "Megan, watch out behind you!" They actually passed well a few times.

In the last minute, Erica had the ball in the clear. Jillian ran just behind her, shouting out encouragement. The goalie was all there was between them and the goal.

Erica kicked hard. The goalie blocked the ball and fell down, and the ball rolled free. Erica passed it to Jillian. Jillian scored the winning goal!

"We did it!" "We won!" "What a team!"

Pam was delighted. "You won because you learned to play together as a team," she told them. "Now you can beat the Cubs next week."

Christian Teamwork

We learned that the Bobcats really wanted to work together. Once they knew that they each had a job to do, they were able to become united and to work as a team.

The early **Christians** also worked as a team. They knew that Jesus wanted them to be united. It was not easy. They had to work toward unity. They prayed, as Jesus prayed, that they might become one with the help of the Holy Spirit.

The First Christians Live as One

The first Christians met together every day at the Temple in Jerusalem. They also gathered daily in their homes—men, women, and children; some rich, some poor. They were people of many nationalities, races, and languages.

They read the **Scriptures**, the written word of God. They listened to the teachings of the **twelve apostles**, those chosen by Jesus to teach and lead his friends and followers. The apostles told them that Jesus wanted them to live in harmony and that Jesus promised to send the Holy Spirit to help them become united.

As they prayed together and ate together, they remembered Jesus and experienced his presence with them. Sharing meals helped them feel united with one another as well as with Jesus.

They shared all they had with one another. Those who had much shared with those who had less. Because they shared all their possessions, there was no needy person among them.

Based on Acts 2:42–47; 4:32–37

We Are a Team

As Catholics, we are part of the team of Jesus' followers. As followers of Jesus, we are called to work and pray for unity among all believers. The Holy Spirit can help us each to do our part.

Activity

Think of the Bobcats, what the apostles taught the early Christians, and of your own experiences in groups. Write in the figures below some of the things that you believe could help a group of people to become united. Then complete the prayer below.

Vocabulary

Scriptures: the written word of God

twelve apostles: those chosen by Jesus to teach and lead his friends and followers

♥ ♥ ♥ ♥ ♥ ♥ ♥ ♥ ♥ ♥ ♥

Dear God,
I belong to a very special team. I am a follower of Jesus. I know that to be a member of Jesus' team I must work for unity. I know that I already _____
_____.

With the help of the Holy Spirit, I will try to _____
_____.

Help me to show that I am truly a member of this very special team. Amen.

We Believe

One of the marks, or signs, of the Catholic Church is that it is one, or united. The Holy Spirit draws Jesus' followers together as brothers and sisters in one Christian family.

Our Parish Community

We can show our team spirit in our **parish** community, where we come together in unity to pray and share stories of our faith. Our Catholic school is an important part of our parish community. We do many things here that show we are part of the parish community. We celebrate school Masses and pray in our classrooms. We talk to one another about what it means for us to be Catholic. We show love for one another and for people who do not even belong to our community. The more we become a team that works and prays together, the more our parish becomes a community.

Activity

As an individual within your parish community, how can you show your team spirit as a member of the team of Jesus' followers?

I belong to the community of _____

_____.

These are some things I can do in my parish community that show that I am part of the parish team.

I can share the sign of peace at Mass.

I can greet people who walk into church with me.

_____

_____.

A United Community

The **Catholic Church** is the Christian community which celebrates the seven sacraments and recognizes the pope and bishops as its leaders. We are united with all Catholics and with those in our parish community when we celebrate the Eucharist.

Our parish is made up of many different kinds of people and families. There are young people and old people, married people and single people. There are people of all races and cultures, from many different places, and of different abilities.

Our parish is made up of children who attend Catholic school and those who attend public school. As members of the Catholic community, we become more united with the help of the Holy Spirit. When Christians are united, they encourage one another to love as Jesus did.

Activity

Our parish family can do many things together to show that we are a united community. What is your parish doing that shows people working, praying, and learning together?

Put a check mark next to each item that shows a way the members of your parish community work, pray, or learn together.

_____ We come together to pray and share the Eucharist at Mass.

_____ We share the school building and classrooms for our religion classes.

_____ We have special Masses for children.

_____ We prepare to receive the sacraments.

_____ We participate in special athletic events.

_____ We help to recycle.

_____ We support and help with special parish events.

Vocabulary

parish: a special community where followers of Jesus come together to pray and share stories of our faith

Catholic Church: the Christian community which celebrates the seven sacraments and recognizes the pope and bishops as its leaders

❤ ❤ ❤ ❤ ❤ ❤ ❤ ❤ ❤ ❤ ❤ ❤ ❤

Unity at Home

Earlier in this chapter, the Bobcats discovered that teamwork takes both leaders and followers. The twelve apostles were good leaders as they taught the early Christian communities. They also prayed to be good followers of Jesus. Just as the Bobcats and early Christians worked to become teams, so must our own families. Working as a team, we can often complete our tasks more easily and quickly.

Activity

Do you remember what makes good leaders and followers? Think about your team of family members as well as your team of schoolmates. As you complete the following statements, include some of the qualities that you have that make each statement true.

I am a good leader because _____.

I am a good follower because _____.

The Unity of Families

Jesus was part of a family, the Holy Family. He worked, prayed, and played with Mary, his mother, and with Joseph. They were united in their love and care for one another.

Jesus is with us in our own families, too. We know through our own experiences that no two families are alike. They may be large or small. They may have both a mother and a father or perhaps a single parent. No matter what our family is like, Jesus is with us and wants us to love and care for one another.

Families come together as Jesus' community, the Church. They gather in times of trouble as well as in times of rejoicing to praise God. They share traditions, customs, blessings, and prayers which nourish the members of a parish family.

Growing in Unity

Jesus calls us to follow the example of unity found among the first Christians. What are some ways Jesus' followers can grow in unity today?

As Catholics, we answer Jesus' call to unity by helping our parishes grow into better communities. Wherever we live in the world, Catholics of different cultures are still united. This unity is shown in our love for Jesus.

- We are all members of the family of Jesus.

- We belong to a united community.

- We celebrate a variety of family and parish customs and practices.

- We participate within our parishes to help people in need.

- We pray and share in the Eucharist.

- We gather together each week.

- We read the Bible and share stories of Jesus with others.

Praying for Unity

Fill in the blanks to complete this prayer of petition for unity.

Lord, we thank you for the example of the first Christians. May your Holy Spirit help us to follow their example at all times and in all the communities to which we belong.

Holy Spirit, we pray for unity in our religion class.

Help us _____.

Holy Spirit, we pray for unity in our school.

Help us _____.

Holy Spirit, we pray for unity in our parish family.

Help us _____.

Holy Spirit, we pray for unity in our homes.

Help us _____.

Holy Spirit, help us encourage one another to live as Jesus wants us to live. Amen.

Chapter Review

Write next to each picture words or phrases that describe how the group represented by the picture can show its unity. You may use any word or phrase more than once.

◄ _____

_____

_____

_____

_____ ►

_____

_____

_____

▲ _____

_____

Fill in the answers to the first two questions.

1. What did the twelve apostles teach the first

Christians? _____

_____

2. What did the first Christians do to grow in

unity? _____

_____

_____

Jesus prays, "Father, may they be one as we are one."
Based on John 17:22

3. Talk about how your school can grow in unity this year.

Our Church Is Holy

Close to God

Diego loved to play soccer from the time his father coached him at home in Bolivia. One Saturday in his new home in Washington, Diego wanted to play soccer, but none of his friends could come to play with him. So he went to sit down under a tree in his backyard. This was his favorite place to go to be alone. It was quiet and peaceful.

His thoughts drifted back to Bolivia. Diego remembered the words his grandmother said to him every time he left the house. "*Vaya con Dios,*" she would say. "Go with God." In good times and in bad times, she would say, "God is always with us." And she believed this with all her heart. For a few minutes, Diego had a feeling that God was there with him, just as his grandmother had said.

"Diego! Let's play soccer!" his friend Alex shouted. "I can come out now."

Did you ever do anything that you thought was a holy thing to do? What was it?

Just then Diego remembered that his mother had asked him to take the morning paper over to Clara, an elderly neighbor, so that she could read it, too.

"Alex," he answered, "I forgot to do something for Mom. I'll be back in a minute!" He ran back to his house to get the paper.

When he gave it to Clara, she smiled at him. "*Gracias,*" she said. "Thanks." As he turned to leave, she added, "*Vaya con Dios!*"

Discuss

1. When and where did Diego feel closest to God?
2. Have you ever felt especially close to God? When? Where?

Holiness Is . . .

The first Christians were **holy** people. Like Jesus, they were close to God and cared about others. They followed the ways that Jesus taught.

Like the first Christians, the Church today is also called to be holy. We pray together at home and in our parishes. We share things and help one another. To be holy is to be close to God, to love God and others, and to do his work in the world.

A Holy People

The Christians in Jerusalem knew how much Jesus had loved the Temple. So every day, they prayed together in the Temple.

"I used to come here often with Jesus," one of them told his friends. "God seemed to be close to us here."

Later, the Christians went back to the house where they met each day. They sat down to eat. After the meal, one of them spoke up.

"Jesus also seemed to bring God close when he was with people in their homes or in the marketplace. And he seemed to bring God's presence near when he was with the sick and the poor."

"Jesus, the Son of God, wants us all to become sons and daughters of God," one of the women added. "He calls us to listen to God's word and to do God's work in the world. Jesus taught us to love our neighbor and to care about anyone who is in need. That's how *we* can be holy, like Jesus."

The group was silent for a moment. Barnabas placed a sack of money on the table. "I just sold my farm," he said. "I will share the money with anyone who is in need."

Like Barnabas, everyone shared whatever they had. They gave praise and thanks for God's goodness. They took bread and wine, blessed them, and shared them in memory of Jesus.

Based on Acts 2:42–47; 4:32–37, 5:11–16

Activity

Find times and places in the story when the first Christians were close to God. List some of them below. Then make a list of the times and places when we are closest to God today.

The first Christians were close to God when _____

_____

_____

_____ .

The Church today is close to God when _____

_____

_____

_____ .

We Believe

One of the marks, or signs, of the Catholic Church is that it is holy. Being holy means to be close to God and to do his work in the world. It means loving God and caring about all people.

Activity

People take opinion polls to find out what others think or feel about something. Here is an opinion poll about holiness. Now that you have learned more about what it means to be holy, take the poll yourself. Put a ✔ in the box that best fits your opinion of holiness.

Opinion Poll	Agree	Disagree	Not Sure
1. People who are holy never have fun.			
2. Hardly anyone is a really holy person.			
3. A holy person cares about others.			
4. A person can become holy by doing ordinary things.			
5. God wants *me* to be a holy person.			
6. Anyone can become a holy person.			

A Holy Church

Jesus' family, the Church, grows closer to God each day and truly cares about all people. We show that we love God when we pray and celebrate the sacraments. Each time we celebrate the Eucharist, we are united with Jesus and the Church. We remember that God our Father, out of love for us, sent Jesus to save us.

The Church also shows love for God by helping and being kind to others. The whole Church throughout the world works together to help people in need, people in our own communities as well as people around the world.

The Church is holy because the people who belong to this community of believers are holy people. On the Feast of All Saints, we pray, "Father, all-powerful and ever-living God, today we rejoice in the holy men and women of every time and place." The holy men and women we honor are called **saints**.

Activity

Write a sentence or draw a picture that tells about something you are doing or have already done that shows you are growing as a holy person.

I Am Holy, Too

Jesus calls us to be holy. The lives of the saints give us many examples of how Christians have answered this call throughout the history of the Church. As you answer Jesus' call to holiness, you, too, could be a saint.

Vocabulary

saints: holy men and women who are honored by the Church because they showed in extraordinary ways that they loved God and others unselfishly

♥ ♥ ♥ ♥ ♥ ♥ ♥ ♥ ♥ ♥ ♥ ♥

Close to God in Prayer

Jesus taught his first followers to pray to God as "Father." We are all God's children. When we pray The Lord's Prayer, also called the Our Father, we pray as sons and daughters of God. In Matthew 6:8b, Jesus says, "Your Father knows what you need before you ask him." Likewise, parents often know what their children need before their children ask. What do we, God's children, ask for when we pray the Our Father?

Activity

Look up Matthew 7:7 in your Bibles. Then decode the Bible words in the following activity to discover three simple things you can do if you want to get closer to God in prayer.

a =   e =    n =   s =

c =   k =    o =

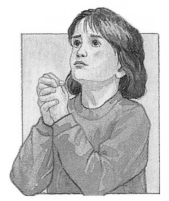

1. "_____ _____ _____ and it will be given to you." Name one thing God can give to you.

   _____

2. "_____ _____ _____ _____ and you will find." Name one special place where you can always find God.

   _____

3. "_____ _____ _____ _____ _____ and the door will be opened to you." Write one thing you could talk to God about the next time you pray.

   _____

Activity

The Holy Spirit is guiding us to live as holy
people. Use the letters in the word *holiness* to tell
what growing in holiness means to you. Two are
done for you.

_____ *H* _____

_____ *O* _____

_____ Ca *L* ling God "Father" _____

_____ *I* _____

_____ *N* _____

_____ Loving oth *E* rs _____

_____ *S* _____

_____ *S* _____

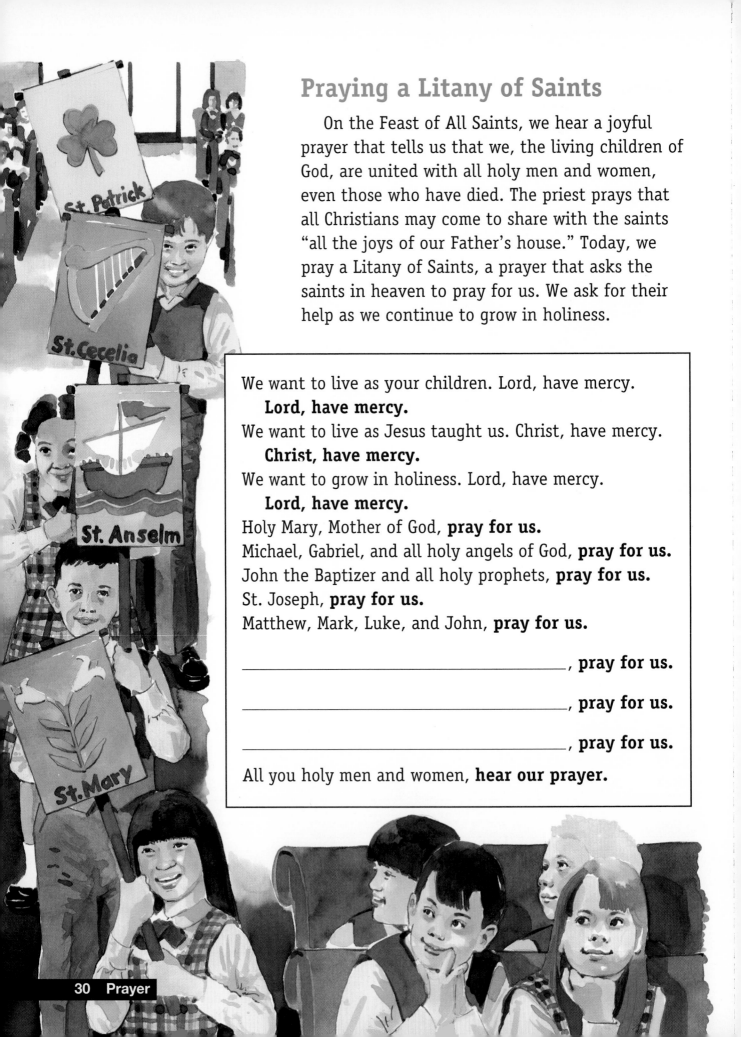

Praying a Litany of Saints

On the Feast of All Saints, we hear a joyful prayer that tells us that we, the living children of God, are united with all holy men and women, even those who have died. The priest prays that all Christians may come to share with the saints "all the joys of our Father's house." Today, we pray a Litany of Saints, a prayer that asks the saints in heaven to pray for us. We ask for their help as we continue to grow in holiness.

We want to live as your children. Lord, have mercy.
Lord, have mercy.
We want to live as Jesus taught us. Christ, have mercy.
Christ, have mercy.
We want to grow in holiness. Lord, have mercy.
Lord, have mercy.
Holy Mary, Mother of God, **pray for us.**
Michael, Gabriel, and all holy angels of God, **pray for us.**
John the Baptizer and all holy prophets, **pray for us.**
St. Joseph, **pray for us.**
Matthew, Mark, Luke, and John, **pray for us.**

_____, **pray for us.**

_____, **pray for us.**

_____, **pray for us.**

All you holy men and women, **hear our prayer.**

Chapter Review

Match each term in Column 2 with its definition in Column 1. Write the correct number from Column 1 on the line next to the term in Column 2.

Column 1

1. Being close to God
2. Promises that God answers prayer
3. Holy men and women we honor at a special feast
4. Helps us grow in holiness
5. What we can call God when we pray

Column 2

_____ saints

_____ Jesus

_____ Holy Spirit

_____ Father

_____ holy

Fill in the answers to the first two questions.

1. What does it mean to be holy? _____

_____

2. How did the first Christians show they were holy? _____

_____

_____

3. Talk about people today who show us what we can do to become holy.

> **You are called to be a holy people.**
> **Based on 1 Corinthians 1:2**

Our Church Is Catholic

3

In what ways are you open to and accepting of others?

A Different World

Nishi stood at the edge of the playground. She felt all tight inside.

She watched the boys and girls playing. She listened to their shouts and laughter. "I wonder what they are saying," she thought.

Nishi started to cry. She thought about her homeland, Japan, on the other side of the world. "I wish I were back home," she thought to herself as she wiped away a tear.

June saw Nishi standing at the edge of the playground. "Mike, look at that girl. She's crying. Do you think she's lonely? Maybe she would like to play."

"Leave her alone," Mike answered. "She's not like us. She looks different and sounds different."

"She is too like us!" June insisted. "She is!"

Nishi saw Mike and June looking at her. She knew they were talking about her. She turned around sadly and began to walk away.

Activity

Write your own ending to the story.

_____

_____

_____

_____

Sometimes I'd like
  To welcome someone
Who's by herself
  Not having fun.
But deep inside
  I am afraid
That I will lose
  The friends I've made.

Jesus and Zacchaeus

As Jesus and his disciples walked along a road in Jericho, a crowd of people gathered around them. The people were anxious to see Jesus. They had heard about all the good things he was doing. Zacchaeus, who was a very short man, wanted to see Jesus, too. So he climbed up into a sycamore tree to see above the crowd.

Jesus saw Zacchaeus up in the tree and said to him, "Zacchaeus, what are you doing up in that tree? Come down here. I want to talk to you. I am coming to visit you at your house today." So Zacchaeus came down and was very happy to greet Jesus. But the crowd became angry. They began to shout loudly, "Why should Jesus go to _his_ house? Zacchaeus is not an honest man. He cheats us when he collects our tax money."

Zacchaeus could see that the crowd was angry. He said to Jesus, "I am so sorry, Jesus. I want to change my life. I will give half of everything I have to the poor. And I will pay back in full all the people I have cheated." Jesus said, "Zacchaeus, you are forgiven."

Based on Luke 19:1–9

Open to All

One evening a group of Christians met in the home of Judith and David in Jerusalem. They ate, sang, and prayed together, as they did every day. They remembered some of the people whom Jesus had helped.

"Jesus once welcomed a Greek woman and healed her sick daughter," Judith said. "And he healed the servant of a Roman."

"He even talked and ate with Samaritans," David added.

"And remember when the Holy Spirit first came?" added Susanna. "People from all over the world were in Jerusalem. Each of them understood the words of the apostles, even though they spoke different languages."

"Jesus taught that all people are sons and daughters of God," said David. "So we are all brothers and sisters."

"You may be right," Susanna answered, "but it is not easy for me to accept people who are different from me."

"The Holy Spirit will help us be open to everyone," Judith assured her.

Based on Matthew 8:5–13; Mark 7:24–30; John 4:4–43; Acts 2:1–13; Galatians 3:26–28

What Being Catholic Means

The first Christians learned from one another that, to be like Jesus, they must welcome everyone who sincerely wanted to belong to their communities. This is what it means to be **catholic**. The word *catholic* means "to be open to the whole world." The Holy Spirit helps us to include persons of all colors, races, ages, and abilities in our lives and in our Church rather than ignore them. The Holy Spirit helps us to accept rather than reject them. This is how we live as daughters and sons of God.

Vocabulary

catholic: open to and accepting of people everywhere

♥ ♥ ♥ ♥ ♥ ♥ ♥ ♥ ♥ ♥ ♥ ♥ ♥

We Believe

One of the marks, or signs, of the Church is that it is catholic. Jesus wants his people, the Church, to welcome and to include people of all kinds, just as he does.

United Yet Different

The Church is one, holy, and catholic. We learned that to be catholic means to be open to people of all kinds. No matter where we live, what we look like, or who we are, the Church is called to welcome us. From the very beginning of the Church, Jesus wanted the Church to be a united community that would include all people and nations.

As Catholics, we welcome and accept people who are different from us in many ways. We are united, but we are not alike in all ways. We share the same belief in Jesus when we celebrate the Eucharist, but we celebrate in a variety of ways. We all sing songs at Mass, but we may sing in different languages. And even when we sing in the same language, we sing many different kinds of songs. Catholics may be different from one another in many ways. Can you think of some other ways that Catholics are different from one another, even though they are united?

Holy Communion in the Byzantine Rite

Easter in Guatemala

Learning to Love All

We who call ourselves Catholics are called to welcome, accept, respect, and be open to all people.

The Catholic Church today is blessed with the special gifts of people of many nations, races, and abilities. Here are some of our brothers and sisters around the world and a prayer to help us all become more open to and accepting of others.

*Spirit of Love,
open our hearts to accept
all people. Give us the strength
we need to be gentle with those
who seem different from us.
Guide all that we think, do,
and say, as we learn to love
everyone, just as Jesus does.
Amen.*

Activity

Describe one way that you can put this prayer into practice. Try to be specific.

_____

_____

_____

Respecting Differences

As members of Jesus' family, the Church, we **respect** the many ways that Catholics around the world pray and celebrate their faith. As brothers and sisters in faith, we believe that our various cultures and customs help to make the Catholic Church a family that truly welcomes everyone. We are happy to see and respect differences among people in our own parishes as well as around the world.

Easter blessing of food in Ukraine

Activity

Think about some of the special ways that your family celebrates holidays and family celebrations. You may want to find out something new about the religious customs in the countries that your family or ancestors come from. Think of some ways you might share one of these with your class or with your parish. On the lines below, write about one prayer or custom. Then share it with your class.

First Communion in Guatemala

When There Is No Respect . . .

Throughout the Church's history, there have been many people who worked hard to bring Jesus' message of unity to all peoples. Oscar Romero, who became the Archbishop of San Salvador in 1977, tried to bring this message to the people of El Salvador.

Most of the people in El Salvador were very poor. A few rich families were in power over the poor families and anyone who tried to help them. Archbishop Romero listened and learned about the problems of the poor people. Having money and power was so important to the rich families that they began to kill or put in jail the priests who were helping the poor. On his radio program, Archbishop Romero began to speak out against this violence. He wanted people to respect each others' rights.

Soon Archbishop Romero became so popular with the poor people that his own life was in danger. The powerful people wanted to kill him because they disagreed with what he was doing. But he did not stop speaking out. He believed that the Church needed him to speak up for the rights of the poor. He believed this was a very important part of being a Catholic Christian. So he continued his work with the poor and continued speaking out for them until March 24, 1980. On that day, he was shot and killed for trying to help the poor people of his country.

Activity

As a group, choose one of the following things to do this year that will help you appreciate the gifts of Catholics different from you.

- Write to a Catholic pen pal in another country.

- Learn a Catholic prayer in a language not your own.

- Put in a class album pictures and articles about Catholics around the world.

Vocabulary

respect: to act with care toward someone or something

❤❤❤❤❤❤❤❤❤❤❤❤

Praying a Litany of Petition

We pray, as Jesus did, that all Christians will be united as they learn to respect one another. We pray that all people will feel welcome in our parish communities. We pray that we can learn to be truly *catholic*.

Let us pray.

For each person in our class, that each of us will know that we are part of the family of God, we pray,
Lord, help us to welcome the strangers among us.

For all the teachers and students of our school, that we will show respect for one another in all that we say and do, we pray,
Lord, help us to welcome the strangers among us.

For our parish family, that we may always be united in our love for Jesus, we pray,
Lord, help us to welcome the strangers among us.

For the people in our community and throughout the world who are not loved as they should be, just because they are different, we pray,
Lord, help us to welcome the strangers among us.

For all those who work toward unity by teaching people ways to respect one another, we pray,
Lord, help us to welcome the strangers among us.

God of all nations, help us to be truly *catholic*. Teach us to be open to people who are different from us. Help us learn to accept them, welcome them, and love them. We pray this in Jesus' name. Amen.

Chapter Review

Use the clues below to fill in the crossword puzzle.

Down

1. A man whom Jesus welcomed

2. Open and accepting of people everywhere

3. The archbishop who helped the poor people of San Salvador

Across

4. The first Christians learned to _____ and accept people who were different from them.

5. To act with care toward someone or something

6. The Holy _____ helps us to accept all people.

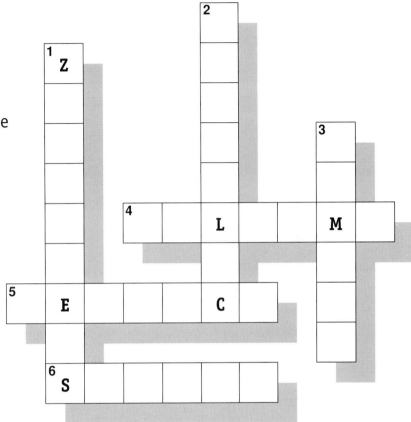

Fill in the answers to the first two questions.

1. What does *catholic* mean? _____

_____

2. Why does the Church welcome all kinds of

people? _____

_____

_____

3. Talk about one thing your class can do to help others feel more welcome in your parish.

**Jesus says,
"I was a stranger
and you
welcomed me."**
Based on
Matthew 25:35b

Our Church Is Apostolic

Tell about a time you were so excited about something that you could not wait to tell your friends all about it.

A Fascinating Cross

"The mail just came," Harry's mom announced. "There's a package here from Angela."

Harry and his younger sister, Molly, ran down the stairs eagerly. Their big sister, Angela, was spending a year in El Salvador as a volunteer teacher.

Their mom quickly opened the package.

"What is it?" Molly asked.

"It looks like a cross," Harry answered. "But it's not like any cross I've ever seen."

Their mom held it up. They examined it carefully. It was made of wood and had brightly painted pictures of people on it.

"That looks like a boy carrying firewood," Molly observed, pointing at one of the paintings.

"Is that a woman carrying a basket of fruit on her head?" asked Harry.

"It sure is," Mom said. "And that looks like a man working in a garden."

"And there's the family dog," Molly noticed.

Then Mom unfolded a note, which was also in the package. "Harry, would you like to read the note from Angela for us?"

Harry read it clearly. "Hi, Mom! Hi, Molly and Harry! I hope you like this cross. It says so much about the faith of the people here. They put pictures on the cross that show the things they do every day. This reminds them that Jesus is with them all the time. I've learned so much from them about what it really means to be a Christian. I miss you all and love you very much. I wish you were here! Angela."

"Let's hang the cross in the living room," Mom said. "It can remind us of Angela and that Jesus is with us here at home and wherever we go."

Telling Others About Jesus

Because we are all different and come from different backgrounds, we learn about Jesus and come to know him in a variety of ways. The apostles lived at the same time as Jesus did. They spent much time with him and so learned about him firsthand. He was their teacher. They told others about Jesus and taught the early Christians how to live as Jesus wanted them to. They spread the good news of Jesus' love for all people by the way they lived and by what they said. We call this good news the **gospel**. Today we learn about Jesus from other Catholics. We learn about the gospel at home, during Mass, and in religion class.

We cannot see or speak to Jesus the way the apostles and early Christians did, but we can still know Jesus and be close to him through our own daily experiences.

We have already learned about three **marks of the Church**—that it is one, holy, and catholic. The fourth mark of the Church is that it is **apostolic**. This means that our Catholic Christian beliefs and ways of living are based on the teachings of Jesus and his apostles. We find these teachings in the Bible.

Vocabulary

gospel: the good news of Jesus' love for all people

marks of the Church: signs of the Church that show it is one, holy, catholic, and apostolic

apostolic: founded on and faithful to the teachings of Jesus and his apostles

♥ ♥ ♥ ♥ ♥ ♥ ♥ ♥ ♥ ♥ ♥ ♥ ♥

We Believe

One of the marks, or signs, of the Catholic Church is that it is apostolic. It is founded on the teachings of Jesus and his apostles. We are called to be apostolic by sharing what we have learned from the apostles and from other Catholics.

Sharing the Good News of Jesus

Philip was sent out by God to share the good news about Jesus. As Philip was walking along a road, a carriage pulled by two large horses began to pass him. He looked up and saw an important man from the country of Ethiopia.

As the carriage passed by, Philip heard the man reading the Scriptures out loud. Philip was very surprised that this man knew about the word of God.

Philip ran and caught up with the carriage. He called out to the man inside, "Do you understand what you are reading?"

"How can I?" the man answered. "Come up and explain it to me." The man invited Philip to sit down beside him.

Philip jumped up into the carriage. Then the man read a few sentences from the Scriptures.

"Please tell me what these words are saying," he said.

"Christians believe they are about Jesus the Christ," Philip explained. "Jesus was a great teacher. He brought God's love to people, especially the poor. God sent him to show us the way to live. His enemies killed him, but God raised him to new life. Jesus loves *you*, too. You can be his follower and friend."

The man was excited. He believed in Jesus. He wanted to become a Christian.

"There's water right here," the man told Philip as they came near to some water. "Could I be baptized?"

Philip and the man jumped down from the carriage. Philip baptized him. Then the man from Ethiopia went happily on his way.

Based on Acts 8:26–38

Activity

We are sometimes called to share the gospel with people who have never even heard of Jesus. Sometimes we share with people who have beliefs that are different from ours. It is especially important at these times to share the gospel by the way we live.

Can you think of some things you could do, rather than say, to show others that you are a Catholic Christian? Draw or write your ideas here.

Activity

When we share the gospel with others, we can help the Church to grow. This is what Jesus told the apostles to do. In Mark 16:15, we read that Jesus told them to go into the whole world to share the good news with everyone. When we share the good news, our **faith** can grow stronger. And we also help others to have faith. Part of what it means to have faith is to believe the good news that Jesus loves us.

Look at each of the following pictures. Read about the way in which each picture shows someone spreading the good news of Jesus' love. What do you see in each picture that also shows that the Church is united, holy, and catholic?

Going halfway around the world to tell people about God's love for them ▼

▲ Taping a TV Mass for people who are too old or sick to go to Mass at their parishes

Teaching a hearing impaired child to say "I love you" in sign language ▼

To the Ends of the Earth

The twelve apostles were sent to spread the gospel message to everyone. Just as crowds of people often gathered to hear Jesus when he taught, the apostles often taught many people about Jesus. Since they were among his closest friends, the apostles knew Jesus best. So people really listened to them. Today, we pray that we will have the courage to share the good news, too.

Jesus, you asked the apostles to go and teach all nations. You asked them to baptize all people in your name. Help us today to be like the apostles. Show us the ways that we can share the good news with one person or with many, with people who are near to us, and with people who are far away. We pray in Jesus' name. Amen.

Vocabulary

faith: the belief that Jesus loves us and our response to God's call

♥ ♥ ♥ ♥ ♥ ♥ ♥ ♥ ♥ ♥ ♥ ♥

Activity

Pretend you are a reporter for *The Apostolic Times*. Use newspapers, magazines, and your own interviews to report on the apostolic activities of the Church today. Print your front-page story below.

THE APOSTOLIC TIMES

Vol. 21 - No. 19   Friday, April 15   30 cents

Witnesses for Jesus

Each of us is called to be a **witness**. We are called to share what we know about Jesus and to live in the ways that Jesus wants us to. Today, our Church leaders remind us that the witness of our lives is very important. When we live faithfully according to the Church's teachings, others will see that Catholics are faithful and loving people.

The apostles traveled long distances through all kinds of weather to spread the gospel to everyone. Like the apostles, many **missionaries** are sent out to spread the gospel throughout the world today. Missionaries, both men and women, often serve God and the Church as teachers and as healthcare workers. They also help people in many lands to live better lives.

Activity

Jesus promised that all who believe in him can do great things with the help of the Holy Spirit. Even though you are not traveling throughout the world, you can still help people to learn about Jesus and to live better lives. What are some ways that you can help?

_____

_____

_____

_____

Vocabulary

witness: one who shares what he or she knows about Jesus and lives in the ways that Jesus wants us to live

missionaries: people who are sent out to spread the gospel throughout the world

♥♥♥♥♥♥♥♥♥♥♥♥♥

Praying a Jesus Meditation

Our prayer today is a Jesus meditation. In this prayer of meditation, we will recall a story about Jesus from the Bible and imagine that we are there in the same place as Jesus.

Close your eyes and listen as your teacher tells the story. After each question, take some time to think about possible answers. Think about what it would be like to meet Jesus, face to face.

Jesus is entering the town of Jericho. He is walking slowly. What does he look like? What is he wearing? Many people are coming to walk with him. They know that he has just helped a blind man to see for the first time in his life. Everyone is very excited and happy that Jesus has come to their town. They all want to get closer to Jesus. Some people are pushing and shoving to get close enough to see his face. Can you see his face? Can you hear what he is saying to the crowd? Is he inviting them to come closer? You have just made your way through the crowd and are close enough for Jesus to hear your voice. Do you have something you would like to say to Jesus? Do you have a question that you think Jesus could answer for you? He is leaning toward you because he knows you want to say something. What do you say? How does he respond? What will you tell your friends about what it was like to meet Jesus?

Chapter Review

missionaries
witness
apostolic
apostles mark
gospel faith

Use the words in the art to complete the sentences.

The fourth _____ of the Church is that it is _____. This means that it is based on the teachings of the _____. Jesus sent out the apostles to be _____. They spread the _____, the good news of Jesus' love for all people, throughout the world. Like the apostles, we are each called to be a _____. We are called to share what we know about Jesus and to live in the ways that Jesus wants us to. When we tell others about Jesus' love for them, we help them to have _____.

Fill in the answers to the first two questions.

1. What is the meaning of *apostolic*? _____

_____

_____

2. How did the apostles share the good news of Jesus? _____

_____

_____

3. Talk about ways that *you* can share the good news of Jesus.

Jesus says,
"Go into the whole world and share the good news with everyone."
Based on
Mark 16:15

In each shape below, describe one or two beliefs or activities that show the Church is living up to each mark of the Church to which it is called.

Holy

_____

_____

_____

_____

One

_____

_____

_____

Catholic

_____

_____

_____

_____

Apostolic

_____

_____

_____

_____

UNIT **1** REVIEW

Use the words hidden in the puzzle to complete these sentences.

1. The first Christians _____ everything they owned.

2. One of the places the first Christians met each day was at the

   _____ .

3. The Scriptures are the written _____ of God.

4. *Holy* means being close to _____ .

5. Welcoming and accepting all _____ is an important part of being catholic.

6. We can _____ others about the good news of Jesus.

7. People noticed how much the first Christians _____ one another.

8. *Catholic* means _____ to people everywhere.

9. Holy men and women are called _____ .

10. To share what you know about Jesus is to be a _____ .

```
X  A  S  A  I  N  T  S
R  T  H  T  E  L  L  M
E  E  A  T  S  G  O  D
W  M  R  W  O  R  V  Q
O  P  E  O  P  L  E  G
R  L  D  R  E  A  D  J
O  E  N  D  N  G  R  E
B  W  I  T  N  E  S  S
```

UNIT **1** REVIEW

Fill in the blanks using the name of one of the four marks of the Church to complete each sentence.

1. _____ means being close to God, loving God and others, and doing God's work in the world.

2. A prayer for unity that Jesus prayed is, "Father, may they be

   _____ as we are one."

3. Our Church is called _____ because it is based on the teachings of the apostles.

4. People who are open to and accepting of anyone from anywhere in the

   world, just as Jesus is, are called _____.

Match the words in Column A with the definitions in Column B.

Column A	Column B
1. Christians	_____ a special community of Jesus' followers who pray together and share stories of faith
2. respect	_____ one who shares about Jesus and lives in his ways
3. parish	_____ the worldwide community of people who believe that Jesus is the Son of God
4. gospel	_____ to act with care toward someone
5. witness	_____ the good news of Jesus' love for all people

WHAT'S a PROBLEM and HOW DO I SOLVE IT?

It is not always easy getting along with friends and members of the family. A disagreement between people is called a *problem.* Problems between people can cause hurt or upset feelings. And the people who cause the problems often hurt as much as the people whose feelings they have hurt. Thinking before acting, thinking of many possible solutions, and choosing a solution that shows you are a follower of Jesus are important parts of being a good problem solver.

STEPS TO PROBLEM SOLVING

Step One: Stop and think.
Step Two: Name the problem.
Step Three: Clarify the goal.
Step Four: Identify possible solutions.
Step Five: Identify possible consequences.
Step Six: Try the best solution.

Activity Jason's Problem

Jason is at the front of the line after recess. Tammy wants to be first and runs ahead of Jason. Jason tells her to move, but she stays in front of him. Can you help Jason solve his problem?

Circle the best response.

1. How is Jason feeling?

   (a) mad   (b) happy   (c) shy

2. What is Jason's problem?

   (a) He wants a longer recess.

   (b) Tammy cut in front of him.

   (c) Tammy won't be his friend.

3. What should Jason do next?

   (a) Tell the teacher.

   (b) Stop and think.

   (c) Push Tammy out of the way.

4. What do you think Jason would like to see happen?

   (a) Jason wants to be first in line.

   (b) Jason wants Tammy to be first.

   (c) Jason wants Tammy to say that she is sorry.

Activity Possible Solutions

Let's assume that Jason's goal is to be first in line again. Write down two or three possible solutions that you think would help Jason accomplish his goal. Be creative!

1. _____

   _____

2. _____

   _____

3. _____

   _____

Look at your solutions. Think about what happens as a result of each solution. We call this the *consequences*. Then choose the solution that you think will help Jason reach his goal and will also show that he is a follower of Jesus. Underline the words that show this is a good solution for a follower of Jesus.

Following Jesus

As followers of Jesus, we need to think about what Jesus taught when we are trying to solve a problem. Remember that Jesus taught us to love our neighbor. One way we can do this is by acting with kindness even when others have been unkind or hurtful to us. Jesus tells us in Mark 12:28–33 that to love God and to love others are the two greatest commandments of all. Remembering this can help us solve many problems.

PRAYER

Jesus, help me choose solutions that show I am your follower. Each time I am making a choice, help me remember your greatest commandments. Help me love my neighbor as I love myself. And help me forgive others when they have hurt me. Amen.

OPENING DOORS
A Take-Home Magazine™

Growing Closer

This Week at
Sacred Heart Parish

MON. – RCIA Catechist Mtg.
TUE. – Social Concerns
　　　　Committee
WED. – Parent Night
SAT. – Fall Harvest
　　　　Festival

TAKE SOME TIME with your family to talk about what makes you a family. Discover again the unique talents and personalities that make up your family as well as those interests and concerns you all share in common. Be grateful for the great gift your family is to you!

READ ALOUD WITH YOUR FAMILY parts of the Sunday parish bulletin. Look for items that encourage members to get to know each other better, to reach out to those in need, to teach, or to become more united in some way. Consider as a family how you might participate in one of these activities.

Answers to page 5: Gathering, welcomes, worship, celebrate, unity

Looking Ahead

THIS IS OUR FAITH, Grade 3, deals with a variety of traditional Catholic teachings. Unit 2 will focus on the most basic affirmation of our creeds. Your child will learn that these creeds focus our minds and hearts on God—Father, Son, and Holy Spirit. The unit will stress that our faith is, above all, a personal relationship with God.

Called to Worship

The power to draw people together has been an earmark of the Church since its beginning. In Greek, the word for "church" is *ekklesia,* which means "gathering together; a people called forth."

We experience this gathering together each time we come to Mass. We assemble as baptized members of the Christian community, the Church. We come together in unity around the Lord's table.

Once gathered, we are called to worship. The Introductory Rites help us move into the spirit of the celebration.

Consider the distinct parts of the Introductory Rites and their particular functions.

you may be familiar. But it serves the American Catholic population in many other ways as well.

The NCCB, established in 1966 in the spirit of Vatican II, brings all the bishops of the United States together to discuss and make decisions on Church matters and to work toward putting their action plans into effect. Acting officially and with authority, the bishops' conference retains a pastoral character.

The NCCB is subdivided into various committees, where much of the work takes place. Among the NCCB's standing committees are Black Catholics, Hispanic Affairs, Liturgy, Missions, Pro-Life Activities, Doctrine, Bishops' Welfare Emergency Relief, Marriage and Family Life, Religious Life and Ministry, and Vocations. The NCCB's ad hoc committees include Evangelization, Campaign for Human Development, Farm Labor, and Catholic Charismatic Renewal.

The bishops' work beyond the local diocese— at regional, state, national, and even international levels—helps to keep American Catholics aware and involved with their universal Church. The hope and courage that our unified efforts give are indeed a welcome sight in the world today!

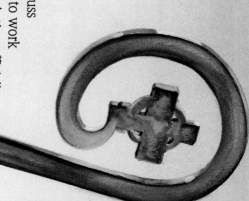

The music and the words of the Gathering Song welcome us and invite us to participate in the celebration.

In the Greeting, the priest and the assembly greet one another and acknowledge the Lord's presence.

In the Penitential Rite, we recognize sin in our lives and humbly accept God's mercy.

In the Gloria, a prayer of praise, we applaud God's goodness.

In the Opening Prayer, we pray a prayer that expresses the theme of the celebration.

We have been gathered and we have been forgiven. We have been greeted and we have begun to pray. Now we, the assembly, are ready to be strengthened by God's word and nourished by the Eucharist.

Being Catholic

Our American Shepherds

AS YOUR THIRD GRADER is learning about how the Church is organized into dioceses, he or she is learning about how bishops serve the Church. As "shepherd" of his diocese, a bishop has a very big responsibility. Locally, a bishop oversees all the parishes of his diocese as teacher, pastoral guide, and administrator. In addition, each bishop tends to the needs of Catholics throughout the country by his participation in the national bishops' conference.

At one time or another, you have probably heard of the National Conference of Catholic Bishops (NCCB). Along with its service agency, the United States Catholic Conference (USCC), the NCCB has produced and published many statements and documents with which

The Christian Family

Spend some time with your child discovering one important part of the Mass that speaks to us of our identity as Catholics. The term catholic means "open to all." The Gathering Rite welcomes us into the celebration regardless of age, race, or nationality and reminds us of the unity we share in Jesus, who is our reason for coming together around the eucharistic table. Read the following with your child.

Every family is made up of different kinds of people. Some family members are older and some are younger. Some work and some go to school. Some like sports and some enjoy music and art. Yet all these different kinds of people make up one family.

The Christian family is made up of many different ages, colors, and talents. Some members are old and some are young. Some are African American and some are Asian. Some are teachers and some are students. Yet all of these different kinds of people belong to the one family of Jesus.

The Gathering Rite is the first part of the Mass that brings us together as the family of Jesus. We remember that we are different people yet members of one family. We have come together to celebrate our unity and to celebrate Jesus, our Brother and Friend, who makes us one.

Unscramble the words below. Use those words to complete a sentence that tells about the Gathering Rite.

rethnigaG   mlweecso   shpiowr   atebrleec   yuint

The _____ Rite _____ all people to _____ God and to _____ our _____ in Jesus.

The next time you go to Mass, look around at the people gathered there. Notice how many different kinds of people make up the family of Jesus in your parish. Thank Jesus for bringing his family together to celebrate the Eucharist.

4   5

UNIT 2

A Believing Community

What are some things you really believe in?

Our Church Believes in God the Father

How do people show you that you can depend on them and trust them, no matter what?

Worries and Fears

Maria was worried. Her mom was away on a business trip. It was a scary feeling, like getting lost at a parade and not remembering the way home. "A hug from Mommy would be the best thing in the world right now," she thought. Maria tried not to let her grandfather know how much she missed her mother.

It had been two days since Maria's mom had left. She had not called. Maria knew where she had gone. The country her mom was visiting seemed so far away. Maria's worries and fears grew. Many questions raced through her mind. "Why hasn't she called me yet?" "Has she forgotten me?" "Doesn't she love me?" "Is Mommy O.K.?"

Maria's grandfather sensed her concern. "Tell me what's wrong, Maria," he said gently.

"Why doesn't Mommy call me? She usually does. Maybe she's hurt. Or maybe she's just too busy." Tears came to Maria's eyes.

Her grandfather put his arms around her. "You're scared and worried," he said. "Your mother has not forgotten you. I know how much she loves you. I'm sure she'll call soon."

Maria wiped her eyes and tried to smile, but her heart still felt sad.

Suddenly the phone rang. Grandfather answered it and then held out the phone to Maria. "It's your mom!" he said.

Maria's mom explained everything. She couldn't call sooner because a storm had cut all telephone lines in the area where she was working. She was fine and would be home in two days. Then they would spend a week of vacation together.

Discuss

1. How would you feel if you were Maria?

2. How did Maria's grandfather help her?

3. What more could you say to help Maria?

Learning to Trust

Jesus taught that whenever we feel alone or afraid, we should remember that God is always with us and cares for us very much. He teaches that God is our loving creator, who cares for all of creation and will never forget us. Just as Maria knew deep down inside that her mother really loved her, we can **trust** that God really loves us, too. Even though God may seem very far away at times, we can trust and believe in his love for us. We can trust and depend upon God as we can trust and depend upon a loving parent.

Vocabulary

trust: to have faith in God's love for us and to believe that he is always with us

★ ★ ★ ★ ★ ★ ★ ★ ★ ★ ★ ★

We Believe

God is our creator. We call God "Father." God takes care of us like a loving parent. God is always faithful to us.

God Is Faithful

One day, Jesus was talking to a large crowd of people. Many of the people had worries and fears. Some worried about money, about having enough food to eat, and about having decent clothes to wear. They wondered if God had forgotten them. Some even began to doubt that God really cared about them.

"Aren't five sparrows sold for just a few pennies?" Jesus asked. "Yet not one of them is forgotten by God. You are worth more than a flock of sparrows!" The people began to feel better as Jesus talked.

Then Jesus pointed to some birds flying above the trees. "Look at the birds," Jesus told them. "God feeds them. God cares for every one of them. How much more important to God are you than the birds! God will never forget you. God is totally **faithful**."

Then Jesus pointed to the flowers that covered the hills. "Look at the lilies," he told the crowd. "If the Father clothes them in such beauty, how much more will he care for you? Stop worrying. Do not be afraid. Trust that God loves you."

Based on Luke 12

Activity

One way to show that we trust God is to bring our concerns and our fears to the Father in prayer. Think about the last time you prayed to God when you were concerned or afraid. Write a prayer to thank God for being faithful to you. Or list some concerns or fears that you could bring to God the next time you pray.

_____

_____

_____

Vocabulary

faithful: someone who is always with us and always caring; someone who is to be trusted and depended upon

★ ★ ★ ★ ★ ★ ★ ★ ★ ★ ★ ★ ★

Calling God "Our Father"

Jesus taught us that when we pray, we can come to God as children and call God "Father," just as Jesus did. We believe that God loves and knows each of us, just as a mother and a father love and know their own children. Decode the Bible words below (Matthew 6:8b) to discover one more thing Jesus taught about God, our Father.

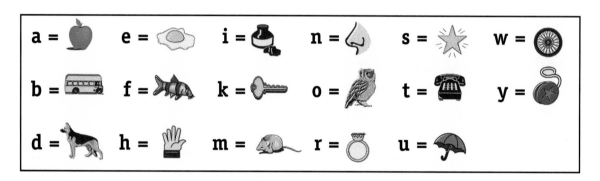

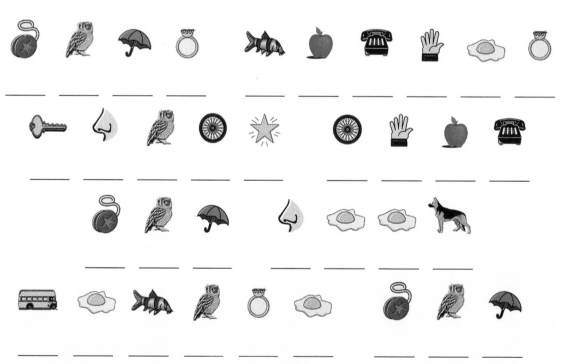

Getting to Know Who God Is

We know that Jesus was very close to God, his Father. Jesus often reminded the people he taught that they could be close to God, too. Jesus promised to send the Holy Spirit to be with us always and to guide and teach us. Whenever we make the Sign of the Cross, we remember that we know God as three distinct Persons: God the Father, God the Son, and God the Holy Spirit. We call this one God in three Persons the **Trinity**.

Jesus told his friends, "I still have many things to tell you, but you will not understand them now. When the Holy Spirit comes, the Spirit will guide you and help you understand." (Based on John 16:12–13). Getting to know God more fully, through the three Persons of the Trinity, will take time. We will grow closer to God as we come to know God as Father, Son, and Holy Spirit.

Vocabulary

Trinity: the one God whom we know as three distinct Persons: God the Father, God the Son, and God the Holy Spirit

★ ★ ★ ★ ★ ★ ★ ★ ★ ★ ★ ★

Activity

Write a story or draw a picture of something you can do to grow closer to God.

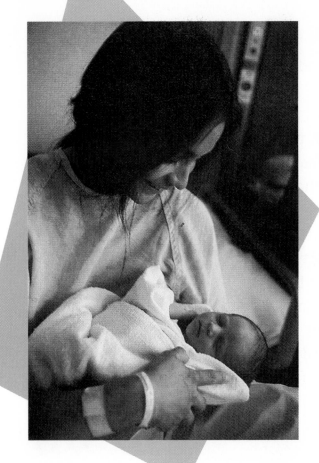

Faithful in Many Ways

We are called to believe that God is faithful to us. *We* are faithful when we trust that God is with us and caring for us wherever we are. We can see God's faithfulness to us in the care that our families and friends show us.

When we were babies, people who loved and cared for us helped us to do many things we could not do for ourselves. They fed us, bathed us, and dressed us. When we remember all the ways that our mothers and fathers, our aunts and uncles, our grandparents, godparents, and others cared for us, we believe that God was caring for us through these special people in our lives.

As children we have often known God's love in the kind actions and words of our friends. Whenever someone has helped us or cared for us in any way, God was caring for us. God cares for us through our friends, our families, our teachers, our pastors, and our parish leaders. God can even care for us through someone we do not know. For example, families sometimes lose everything they have in a fire, a hurricane, or another kind of disaster. People whom these families do not know—people from all over the world—may send them food, clothing, and money.

We Are Faithful, Too!

Just as we can know God's faithfulness through the kindness of others, others can know God's faithfulness through *our* kindness. One way we can show that we are thankful to God for being faithful to us is by our kind words and actions toward others. When we live as God wants us to live and help others to see his love, we can all grow closer to him. The way we speak and act toward others is an important part of our relationship with God. We can also show that we are faithful by praying and by celebrating the Eucharist.

Activity

Write sentences below to tell about some ways that you can be a faithful person. Begin each sentence with a different letter of the word *faithful*. Some sentences have been done for you.

F eed a hungry person. _____

A _____

I _____

T _____

H elp a friend. _____

F _____

U _____

L _____

Praying with Sign Language

Read the words from Isaiah 49. They remind us of God's faithfulness to us. On one of the hands in the picture, write your name. Remember that God will never forget *you!* On the other hand, write the name of someone you love and trust. Thank God for that person. Then pray the prayer below, using sign language, to express your trust in God.

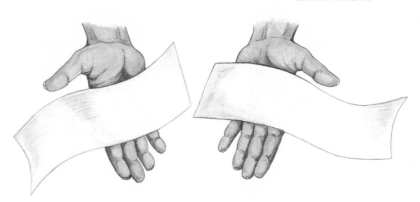

*"I will **not forget** you...I have written your name on the palms of my hands"*

Isaiah 49:15:76

God

I place

my

life

in your

hands

Leader: When I am lonely or afraid,

All: God, I place my life in your hands.

Leader: When I am worried or upset,

All: God, I place my life in your hands.

Leader: When I am happy or excited,

All: God, I place my life in your hands.

Leader: God, we trust in your goodness and love. We thank you in the name of Jesus.

All: Amen.

Chapter Review

Unscramble the word that follows each sentence. Then use the words to complete the sentences.

1. Jesus taught us that God will _____ be with us.

   | lwasay |

2. As Catholics, we believe that God is

   _____.

   | luifathf |

3. We can come to God as children and call God

   _____.

   | erFtha |

4. We can _____ that God will always love us and be with us.

   | ustrt |

5. The _____ is one God in three Persons.

   | yintrTi |

Fill in the answers to the first two questions.

1. What does *faithful* mean? _____

   _____

   _____

2. Why did Jesus tell the story of the birds and

   lilies? _____

   _____

3. Talk about ways we can show our faith in God.

God says, "Can a mother forget her baby or not care about her child? I will never forget you."
Based on Isaiah 49:15

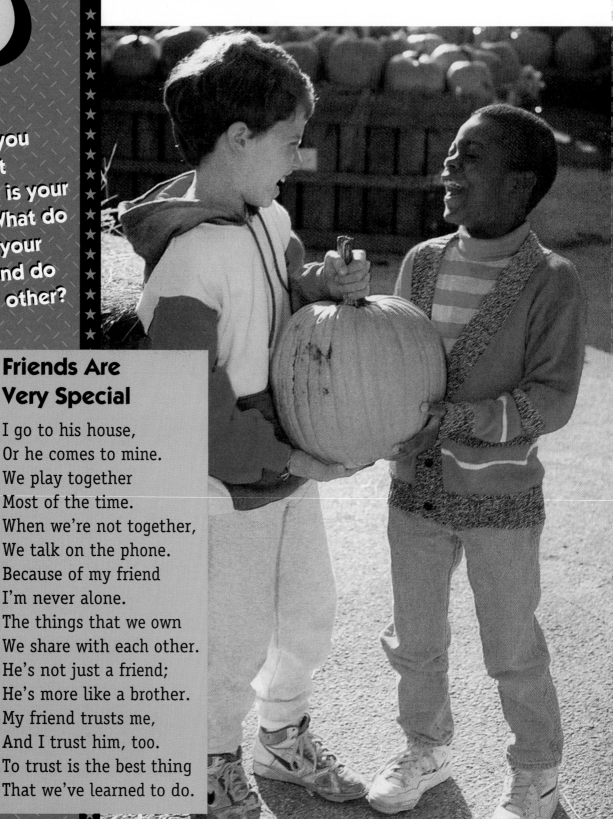

6

Our Church Believes in Jesus Christ

How can you know that someone is your friend? What do you and your best friend do for each other?

Friends Are Very Special

I go to his house,
Or he comes to mine.
We play together
Most of the time.
When we're not together,
We talk on the phone.
Because of my friend
I'm never alone.
The things that we own
We share with each other.
He's not just a friend;
He's more like a brother.
My friend trusts me,
And I trust him, too.
To trust is the best thing
That we've learned to do.

Friends Forever

David was a young shepherd boy who believed he could fight the Philistine giant named Goliath and win! Goliath had insulted David's people, the Israelites. David's people were frightened. But David had so much faith and trust in God that he asked King Saul to let him fight Goliath all by himself.

Using only a slingshot, David killed Goliath. Saul was very impressed. Saul took David into his home as his own son. Saul's son Jonathan became David's best friend. Jonathan and David grew to love each other as brothers.

Saul asked David to lead many battles, and David won them all. This made Saul very happy, but only for a short time. David became very popular with the people. This made Saul jealous and angry. Saul wanted to destroy David, so he sent him into battle after battle, hoping that David would be killed. But David always won because the Lord was with him.

One day, Saul told Jonathan of his plan to kill David. Jonathan warned David about Saul's plans. Jonathan and David made secret plans to keep David safe.

Soon the day came when Saul planned to kill David. David knew that he had to leave. Jonathan and David were very sad, but they knew that they would keep their promise to be friends forever.

Based on 1 Samuel 17–20

Discuss

1. What helped David to be so brave in his battle with Goliath?

2. How did Jonathan help save David's life?

3. In what ways have you shown that you trusted a friend?

Jesus and His Friends

The sun was rising over the lake. Jesus' friends rowed their boat toward shore. They were sad. It was just a few days after Jesus' death. They really missed their friend Jesus.

"Did you catch any fish?" a man called out from the misty shore. "No," they answered.

"Throw the net over the right side of the boat," the man told them with great confidence.

They dropped the net into the dark waters. It filled with fish. Then John recognized the man on the shore. "It is the Lord!" he shouted.

Peter, one of the twelve apostles, was so excited to see Jesus that he dove in and swam ashore. John and the others rowed the boat in with the net full of fish. They, too, were eager to be with Jesus again.

As they secured the boat, they saw a charcoal fire with some fish on it and bread.

"Bring some of the fish you just caught," Jesus told them. He knew they were hungry.

When breakfast was ready, Jesus invited them to sit around the fire. "Come and eat your meal," he said. "It is so good to be with such faithful friends." Jesus' friends came quickly.

They sat down and ate together. They talked and laughed. They were happy to be with Jesus again. He had risen from the dead. He was with them. He was their best friend.

Based on John 21:1–14

Jesus, the Son of God

The apostles loved Jesus very much. He had done so much for them. He was their friend and their teacher. He loved them and taught them to love one another. Before Jesus suffered and died for them, he promised to be with them always and to send the Holy Spirit. After his **resurrection**, when he rose from death to new life, Jesus kept his promise.

Jesus, the Son of God, is always with us, too. He is our best friend, and he loves us very much. He shares in our sadness and our joys. Jesus gives us himself in the Eucharist. He teaches us how to live and how to love.

Vocabulary

resurrection: Jesus' rising from death to new life

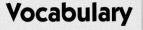

We Believe

Jesus, the Son of God, is always with us. He rose from death to new life. He is our friend forever.

Activity

Look at the pictures. Write in each space what you think one friend is saying to the other.

Christian Friendship in Action

In John 15:14, Jesus says, "You are my friends if you do what I command you." We are called to be a friend to Jesus and to others. We can show others that we are friends of Jesus by trying to follow Jesus' example and teachings. To be the kind of friend that Jesus is, we can listen to our friends when they are sad and we can be happy when they are happy. When we share both our joys and our sadness with one another, we share Christian friendship.

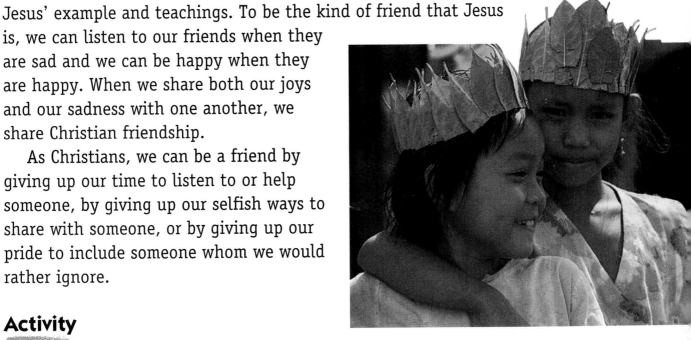

As Christians, we can be a friend by giving up our time to listen to or help someone, by giving up our selfish ways to share with someone, or by giving up our pride to include someone whom we would rather ignore.

Activity

When we follow Jesus' example of doing good things for others, we are reaching out in Christian friendship. Place an **X** beside each statement that shows what it means to be a true friend and follower of Jesus.

_____ I can offer to rake leaves, mow the lawn, or shovel snow for my neighbors.

_____ I can invite someone new to my house.

_____ I can ask a new boy or girl to join our game.

_____ I can decide not to take time to comfort others when they are sad or hurting.

_____ I can help someone with his or her work.

_____ I can ignore someone who wants to play in our game.

_____ I can share my lunch or snack with someone who forgot to bring lunch or with someone who is hungry.

_____ I can walk away from people who need my help.

Getting to Know Jesus

When we think about our closest friends, we often think about the time we spend together and the fun things we do. We talk to some of them on the telephone. We write letters to friends who live far away. We tell our best friends what is happening in our lives and how we feel about things. And if we were introducing our best friend to someone for the first time, we would have so many wonderful things to say.

Some people know many things about Jesus because they have read Bible stories about him. Or they may have heard other people talk about Jesus. Christians often talk to Jesus when they pray. Christians believe that Jesus is with them all the time. Christians know that to follow Jesus means not only to act like Jesus but also to walk with Jesus every day of their lives. Christians know Jesus as a close friend who is faithful to them.

Jesus said, "I am the way and the truth and the life. No one comes to the Father except through me. If you know me, then you will also know my Father" (John 14:6–7). We can grow closer to God by growing closer to Jesus. And we can grow closer to Jesus by sharing in a special friendship with him.

Discuss

1. What are some ways that we can learn about Jesus, our friend?

2. What do you think it means to follow Jesus?

3. How can knowing Jesus as a friend help us to pray?

Activity

Jesus is our friend. Good friends know each other. They like to be together and talk together.

We can get to know Jesus better as we read or listen to the Scriptures. We can also listen to Jesus speak to us when we pray. We also share with Jesus our own joys and concerns. What do you know and like about Jesus?

WALKING WITH JESUS

What I like most about Jesus is _____

_____.

My favorite story about Jesus is _____

_____.

The words of Jesus I like best are _____

_____.

When I am with Jesus, I can pray the words _____

_____.

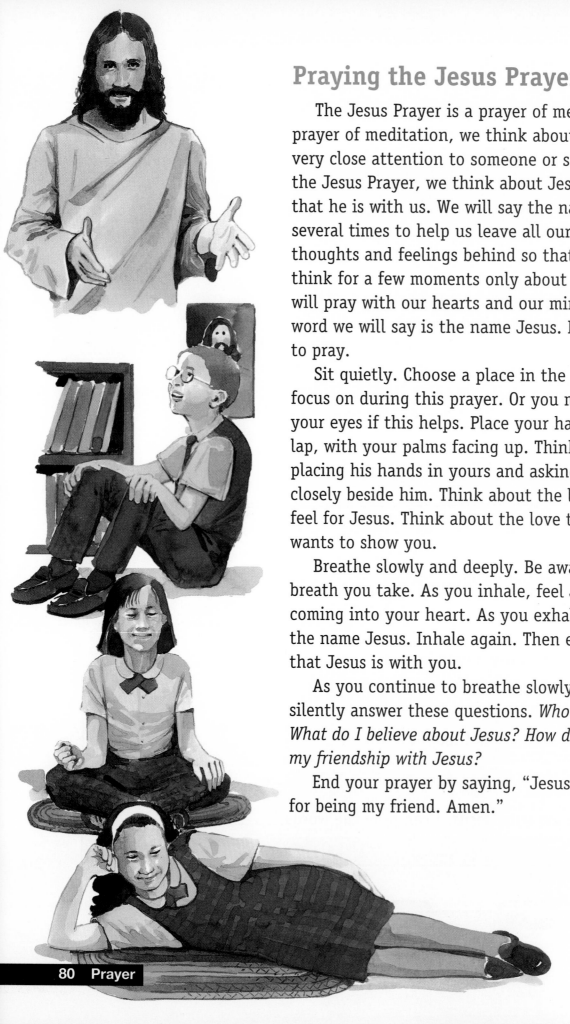

Praying the Jesus Prayer

The Jesus Prayer is a prayer of meditation. In a prayer of meditation, we think about and pay very close attention to someone or something. In the Jesus Prayer, we think about Jesus, believing that he is with us. We will say the name Jesus several times to help us leave all our other thoughts and feelings behind so that we can think for a few moments only about Jesus. We will pray with our hearts and our minds. The only word we will say is the name Jesus. Let us begin to pray.

Sit quietly. Choose a place in the classroom to focus on during this prayer. Or you may close your eyes if this helps. Place your hands in your lap, with your palms facing up. Think about Jesus placing his hands in yours and asking you to walk closely beside him. Think about the love that you feel for Jesus. Think about the love that Jesus wants to show you.

Breathe slowly and deeply. Be aware of each breath you take. As you inhale, feel Jesus' love coming into your heart. As you exhale, softly say the name Jesus. Inhale again. Then exhale. Know that Jesus is with you.

As you continue to breathe slowly and deeply, silently answer these questions. *Who is Jesus? What do I believe about Jesus? How do I feel about my friendship with Jesus?*

End your prayer by saying, "Jesus, thank you for being my friend. Amen."

Chapter Review

Use the clues below to fill in the crossword puzzle.

Down

1. Friends of Jesus live according to his example and _____.
3. One of the twelve apostles who was fishing when he met Jesus again
4. Another one of the twelve apostles
6. He killed Goliath with a slingshot and became Jonathan's best friend.

Across

2. Jesus' friends try to follow his _____ of doing good things for others.
5. Jesus is the _____ of God.
7. He was a true friend to David.
8. Jesus' rising from death to new life

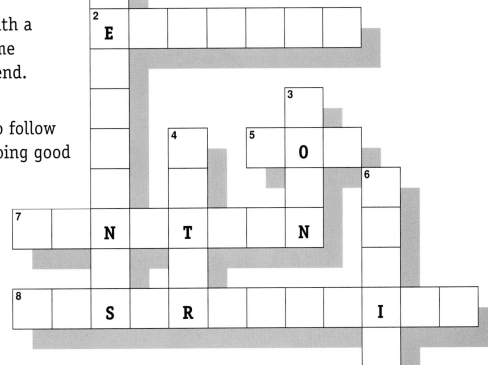

Fill in the answers to the first two questions.

1. What does *resurrection* mean? _____

_____

2. How does Jesus show us that he is our friend?

_____

_____

_____

3. Talk about how you can become a better friend of Jesus.

Jesus says, "You are my friends."
Based on John 15:14

Our Church Believes in the Holy Spirit

When you are not sure you can do something that you very much want to do, who or what helps you most?

Allison's Dream

Allison often dreamed of being a dancer. But when she woke up each morning, she could still feel some pain in her right leg. "I'll never be able to dance," she would say softly.

Allison had been in a car accident when she was six. Her leg had been badly hurt. She walked with a limp.

Miss Burke knew how much Allison wanted to be a dancer. She also knew how hard it would be for Allison to dance well. But she believed Allison had the inner power to make her dream come true.

Day after day, Miss Burke would say, "You can do it, Allison. I know you can. Let's try this move. Watch closely how I do it. Then do the same move as best you can."

Allison slowly began to believe in herself. "I can do it," she began to tell herself as she tried each new step. But sometimes she would lose control and fall. Sometimes it was so hard that she wanted to give up.

Months went by. Miss Burke coached Allison every afternoon. "You *are* a dancer," Miss Burke would say. "Never doubt your dream. You can do it!"

At the end of the year, the dance studio had a program for parents. Allison's dad sat in the front row. Miss Burke watched the dance from the side of the stage. Allison had only a small part in the dance, but she danced her part well.

When she came out to take a bow, everyone stood up and cheered. They knew how hard she had worked to reach her dream. She truly was a dancer!

Discuss

1. Why did Allison's dream to be a dancer seem impossible at times?

2. What helped Allison to keep on trying?

3. What dreams do you have that will take courage to work toward?

The Disciples' Fears

Like Allison, Jesus' disciples thought they would never be able to do something that they were encouraged to do. Jesus had told his disciples to tell others about him. But after Jesus was arrested, the disciples were afraid. They did not dare tell people about Jesus. They had seen what happened to Jesus. He was beaten and crucified. They feared this would also happen to them.

The disciples remembered that Jesus had promised to send the Holy Spirit to give them the power to do things they never thought they could do. Confused and afraid, the disciples gathered together in a house to pray.

Filled with the Spirit ~~~~~

Suddenly, all over the house, there was a noise like a strong wind. It seemed as if tongues of fire blazed above each of the disciples. They were filled with the Holy Spirit. They began at once to talk and praise God in different languages.

The disciples felt a new strength inside them. They were full of joy and peace. Now they could do what they had been afraid to do. They opened the doors of the house and went out to tell the people about Jesus.

A large crowd of people from many different countries listened. They were amazed at what they heard and that each one heard the disciples speaking the language of his or her own country. Then Peter stood up and spoke to the whole crowd.

"I want to tell you about Jesus," Peter said. "Jesus went about doing good for everyone. He cared especially for the poor and suffering. Jesus loved people so much that he willingly died for them. But after he was buried, God raised him up. Believe in Jesus. Change your lives. Be baptized, and you, too, will receive the gift of the Holy Spirit."

Many people were excited after they heard Peter's words. More than three thousand people were baptized that day and became followers of Jesus.

Based on Acts 2:1–41

The Day of Pentecost

The day Jesus' first disciples received the Holy Spirit is called **Pentecost**. The Spirit changed their sadness into joy and their fear into hope. The Spirit filled them with new life and gave them courage to share Jesus with others. This new life filled all the people who believed in Jesus, and the community of believers began to meet together to share this new life. Pentecost marked the beginning of the life of the Church. This is why Pentecost is sometimes called the birthday of the Church.

Vocabulary

Pentecost: the birthday of the Church; the day on which Jesus' first disciples received the gift of the Holy Spirit

★ ★ ★ ★ ★ ★ ★ ★ ★ ★ ★ ★

The Spirit Gives Us Courage

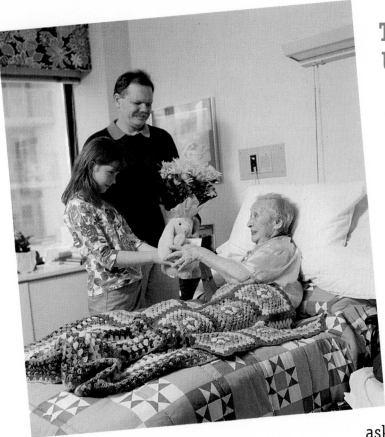

The Holy Spirit continues to give life to the Church and to each of us today. As our helper and guide, the Spirit gives each of us the power to do things we never thought we could do. Just as the disciples were given the courage to tell others about Jesus, we are also given the courage to live as friends and followers of Jesus.

Following Jesus in all that we do and say is not always easy. When we stop to think about the decisions we must make, we can ask the Holy Spirit to guide us in making the best decisions. Sometimes we know what the best decision is, but we do not have the courage to make that decision. For example, we know that Jesus wants us to make choices that show we care for others. But we may consider choosing to act differently or not at all.

Discuss

1. Have you ever made a decision to do something that would give someone the message that you did not care about that person? What happened?

2. What is the most courageous decision you have ever made?

3. Who or what helped you make that decision?

Spirit-Filled Decisions

When we pray, we can ask the Holy Spirit to guide the decisions that we make each day as we try to live as Catholic Christians. We can pray at the beginning of each day for such guidance. This helps to remind us that the Spirit is always with us, all day long. This helps us to make the most caring choices throughout each day.

Activity

Place an **X** before each sentence below that shows that the Holy Spirit is guiding someone to make a caring choice. Then read the sentences again. Circle three of the caring choices that are the hardest for you to make.

_____ "I promised not to tell this to anyone, but I'll tell you anyway."

_____ "I can help with that, Mom."

_____ "No, I'm too busy watching television."

_____ "It's not my turn. I did it yesterday."

_____ "That's okay. I'll take out the garbage."

_____ "Figure it out yourself."

_____ "I can teach you how to do that."

_____ "I don't care. I want to play here."

_____ "I can play in my room if you want to rest."

_____ "I'll play that game with you."

_____ "I don't want to. It's boring."

_____ "I'm sorry I said that."

_____ "Give me that. It's mine."

We Believe

Jesus gives the Church —the community of believers—the gift of the Holy Spirit to be with us as our helper and guide. The Holy Spirit gives us courage and power to do difficult things and to share Jesus with others.

Signs of the Spirit

We are called to open our hearts to receive the Holy Spirit as our helper and guide in living as followers of Jesus.

Signs are used to remind us of the Holy Spirit's activity in our lives. One sign used by the Church is wind, or breath. It reminds us that the Holy Spirit fills us with life. Another sign, fire, reminds us that the Holy Spirit fills us with the warmth of God's love.

Native Americans also believe that wind, or breath, gives life. They believe that the wind carries our thoughts and prayers to God. They say special prayers called "giveaway" prayers to give thanks for all the blessings of nature.

Black Elk's vision of the blooming sacred tree of life

*We give away our thanks
    to the sun
For sending light
    to help our food grow.
We give away our thanks
    to the seas
For giving away their waters
    to refresh us.*

Images of the Spirit

As the Third Person of the Trinity, the Holy Spirit has always been with us. In the Bible, the Holy Spirit is made known to us in many ways—as a helper, as a guide, in wind, and in fire. We can also read about the Spirit at Jesus' baptism. "After all the people had been baptized and Jesus also had been baptized and was praying, heaven was opened and the holy Spirit descended upon him in bodily form like a dove. And a voice came from heaven, 'You are my beloved Son; with you I am well pleased" (Luke 3:21–22). We sometimes see a dove on a banner or on other decorations in our churches, especially on Pentecost Sunday. A dove is often used as a symbol for the Holy Spirit. We may also see this image of the Spirit at a Baptism.

In the story of Pentecost the Holy Spirit is described as a "strong wind" and as "tongues of fire." This is why many parishes show a flame of fire on parish bulletins or banners on special occasions.

In the Bible, the Holy Spirit has many names as well as images. In John 14:26, Jesus called the Holy Spirit our "Advocate," which means one who comforts or gives courage. The Holy Spirit would comfort the disciples when Jesus died and give them courage.

Activity

Write a prayer to the Holy Spirit. Ask the Holy Spirit to show you more signs of the Spirit that can help you live as a friend and follower of Jesus.

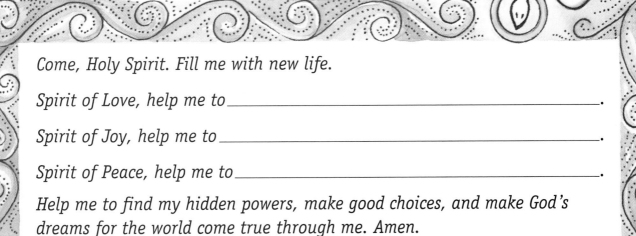

Come, Holy Spirit. Fill me with new life.

Spirit of Love, help me to _____.

Spirit of Joy, help me to _____.

Spirit of Peace, help me to _____.

Help me to find my hidden powers, make good choices, and make God's dreams for the world come true through me. Amen.

Praying a Native American Prayer

The Holy Spirit can be seen and known in so many ways. We pray today that the Holy Spirit will continue to fill our lives and our world. With our Native American brothers and sisters, we pray our own "giveaway" prayer to give thanks for the many signs of the Spirit that help to make our faith stronger. Write your own prayers of thanks to the Holy Spirit.

We give away our thanks for the wind because _____

_____.

We give away our thanks for fire because _____

_____.

We give away our thanks to the Holy Spirit for helping us when _____

_____.

We give away our thanks to the Holy Spirit for guiding us when _____

_____.

We give away our thanks to the Holy Spirit for giving us courage when

_____.

We give away our thanks to the Holy Spirit for always being with us. Amen.

Chapter Review

Before each definition in Column A, write the letter of the word from Column B.

Column A

Column B

_____ **1.** The Third Person of the Trinity

a. dove

_____ **2.** The birthday of the Church

b. Pentecost

_____ **3.** Two ways the Holy Spirit is with us today

c. wind and fire

_____ **4.** What the disciples were doing when the
Holy Spirit came

d. Holy Spirit

e. praying

_____ **5.** The image of the Holy Spirit at
Jesus' baptism

f. giveaway prayer

_____ **6.** A Native American prayer of thanks

g. helper and guide

_____ **7.** Images of the Holy Spirit at Pentecost

Fill in the answers to the first two questions.

1. What is Pentecost? _____

_____

_____

2. How does the Holy Spirit help us today? _____

_____

_____

3. Talk about some signs of the Spirit that you
see and appreciate in one another.

**The Spirit of
Christ lives in you.**
Based on Romans 8:9–10

Our Church Has Creeds

What are three things you strongly believe in? Where do these beliefs come from?

We C.A.N. Make a Difference

Suzie and Elisa were excited. They had decided to start a club to improve the environment. They were now working out their plans at Elisa's house.

"Whom could we invite into our club?" Suzie asked.

"We could start with Sylvia, Pat, and Lois," Elisa suggested. "And maybe Luke and Chang. Then others will *want* to join our club."

"But what will we call ourselves?" asked Suzie.

"Let's name ourselves the Cougars, after our school mascot!" said Elisa.

"How about the C.A.N. Plus Club? The letters can stand for '**C**ougars **A**ct **N**ow.' And our name would show that we *can* make a difference by taking action now."

"And that recycling *cans* is only the first step."

"We could put up signs telling people why recycling is so important."

"And help people learn what other things to put aside for recycling."

"How about planting trees and flowers?"

"And sweeping up trash."

Suzie and Elisa named many other projects.

"Let's go and write down all that the C.A.N. Plus Club stands for before we forget," Suzie suggested.

They spent the rest of the evening printing out their club's creed very neatly. "Now we can invite others to join our club," Suzie said. "Tomorrow we'll start!"

Activity

Think about the groups you belong to and the activities you most enjoy. What do your activities tell about the kind of person you are and what you stand for?

A group I belong to is _____.

One of my favorite activities is _____.

My favorite activities show that I am _____.

Jesus' Followers Knew What They Stood For

Jesus' followers knew what they stood for—the same things that Jesus taught and lived. Jesus told his disciples, "This is how all will know that you are my disciples, if you have love for one another" (John 13:35). Jesus told his followers that the most important sign of the Christian community is the love that Christians show for one another.

The Apostles' Creed ～～～

It is several hundred years after Pentecost. In the great city of Rome, a group of Christians are meeting in someone's home. They pray together and read from the Scriptures.

"It is so good for us to come together like this," Timothy says. "Our faith grows stronger each time we meet."

"We must never forget all that we have come to understand," Paula urges. "Let's renew our faith now before we go home."

Quietly but confidently, they said their creed.

The Trinity in Our Creeds

Our belief in the Trinity is an important part of all of our creeds. Each creed begins by stating our belief in God the Father, the First Person of the Trinity. We can remember that this is the first part of each creed because God the Father is the creator of all things, and creation was the beginning of all of God's wonderful works.

The second part of each creed states our belief in Jesus, the Second Person of the Trinity. We believe that Jesus is God. We believe that Jesus is both divine and human. When we say that Jesus is human, we are saying that he is like us. When we say that Jesus is divine, we are saying that he is God. This is what makes Jesus different from all other teachers and leaders who bring God's love to us.

The third part of each creed states our belief in the Holy Spirit, the Third Person of the Trinity. We believe that the Holy Spirit is the one whom Jesus promised would be with us always. We believe that the Holy Spirit is God, who is alive in the Church today and in the hearts of all believers.

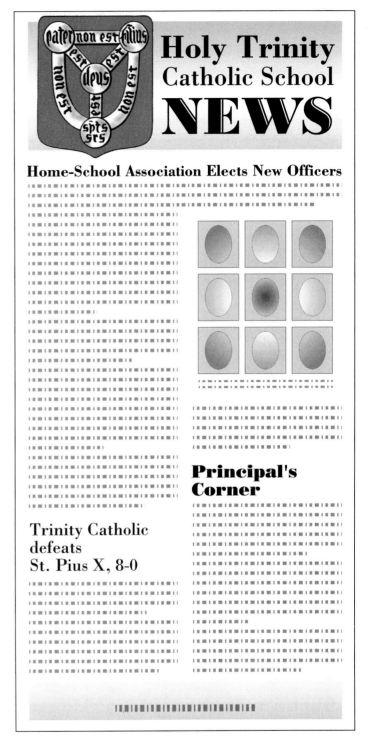

Holy Trinity Catholic School NEWS

Home-School Association Elects New Officers

Trinity Catholic defeats St. Pius X, 8-0

Principal's Corner

One Faith, Many Creeds

Throughout history we have come together to share our faith. Creeds are important because they express what we believe as a Church community. The Church uses different creeds at different times, but each creed expresses our belief in the Three Persons of the Trinity, in the Church, and in eternal life.

There are several different creeds. Each time we celebrate Baptism, or remember the promises made at Baptism, we use a form called the baptismal creed, or Renewal of Baptismal Promises. We also use this form at the Easter Vigil and at the Easter Sunday Mass because we renew our baptismal promises at these celebrations. We believe that Baptism celebrates the beginning of

our faith. When we were baptized, our parents and godparents were asked questions that began with the words, "Do you believe?" As they answered "I do" to each question, they expressed their own faith. We also express our faith each time we answer these questions by saying, "I do."

The Nicene Creed is the creed that we usually say at Mass. It lists the primary beliefs of our faith as people of God and as members of the Catholic Church. Each statement of faith begins with the words "*We* believe." This reminds us that we are united in our faith with our parish families and with Catholics throughout the world.

The Apostles' Creed, based on the teachings of the apostles, is often used in Masses for children. In this shorter creed, we begin each statement of faith with the words, "*I believe.*" This reminds us that our faith comes from within the heart of each believer.

Activity

Use your own words to complete the sentences.

1. We believe that God is faithful to us when _____

_____

_____.

2. We believe that Jesus is our friend and brother when _____

_____

_____.

3. We believe that the Holy Spirit is our helper and guide when

_____

_____.

4. We believe that the Catholic Church is a faithful

Church when _____

_____.

Praying a Blessing

Leader: Let us pray in the name of the Father, Son, and Holy Spirit. (All make the Sign of the Cross.)

All: Amen.

Reader 1: God the Father almighty, who created heaven and earth,

All: We praise you, O God.

Reader 2: Jesus Christ, our Lord, who was conceived by the Holy Spirit, suffered and died for us, has risen, and will come again,

All: We praise you, O God.

Reader 3: Holy Spirit, who gives life to the Church and courage to all believers,

All: We praise you, O God.

Leader: Lord God, we worship you as Father, Son, and Holy Spirit. We pray that you will always keep your Church strong in faith.

All: Amen.

Leader: A reading from the second letter of Paul to the Corinthians: Goodbye, my friends. Listen to all I have said. Live peacefully with one another. Encourage one another. Show the world that you are a community of love. Greet one another warmly. I will pray for you, that the grace of our Lord Jesus Christ, the love of God the Father, and the fellowship of the Holy Spirit will always be with all of you.

(Based on 2 Corinthians 13:11–13)

The word of the Lord.

All: Thanks be to God.

Leader: Let us extend our hands in blessing to one another.

Group 1: May our Lord bless you and keep you faithful always.

Group 2: In the name of the Father, Son, and Holy Spirit. Amen.

Group 2: May our Lord bless you and keep you faithful always.

Group 1: In the name of the Father, Son, and Holy Spirit. Amen.

Chapter Review

Draw a line from each Person of the Trinity in Column A to the matching phrase in Column B.

Column A	Column B
God the Father	came at Pentecost
Jesus	sent Jesus to save us
The Holy Spirit	rose from the dead

List four things you say you believe in when you say the Apostles' Creed.

1. _____

2. _____

3. _____

4. _____

Fill in the answers to the first two questions.

1. What is the Apostles' Creed? _____

_____

_____

2. What are some other creeds of the Church?

_____

_____

Remain faithful to what you believe.
Based on 2 Timothy 3:14

3. Talk about which parts of the creeds you would like to learn more about.

Define *creed* on the lines in the scroll. Complete the chart by describing the beliefs you profess about the Father, Jesus, and the Holy Spirit.

CREED

_____
_____
_____
_____
_____
_____
_____
_____

GOD

_____
_____
_____
_____
_____

_____   _____
_____   _____
_____   _____
_____   _____
_____   _____

UNIT **2** REVIEW

Place an X before each true sentence. Correct any false sentences by rewriting them.

1. _____ Jesus taught that birds are more important to God than people are.

2. _____ God the Father is always faithful to us.

3. _____ Creeds summarize the beliefs of the Church.

4. _____ The day the disciples received the Holy Spirit is called Christmas Day.

5. _____ The resurrection of Jesus is his rising from death to new life.

Place an X before each statement that expresses a Catholic belief.

1. _____ God loves me.

2. _____ I have to be grown up before I can be a friend of Jesus.

3. _____ The Holy Spirit gives life to the Church and to me.

4. _____ I will rise from death to new life.

5. _____ The Apostles' Creed lists the names of the twelve apostles.

6. _____ Jesus will come again.

7. _____ I can depend upon God.

8. _____ Jesus is human only, not divine.

9. _____ The dove is an image of Jesus in the Bible.

10. _____ The Holy Spirit gives us courage.

Circle the correct letter to complete each sentence.

1. Jesus promised to send the Holy Spirit to _____ and guide us.
(a) frighten   (b) help   (c) believe

2. Jesus taught that God, our Father, _____ us.
(a) cares for   (b) forgets   (c) is afraid of

3. Jesus, the _____ of God, is always with us.
(a) Father   (b) Son   (c) Holy Spirit

4. _____ is called the birthday of the Church.
(a) Easter   (b) Christmas   (c) Pentecost

5. I believe in God, the Father _____ , creator of heaven and earth.
(a) almighty   (b) priest   (c) sometimes

Find the words about the Holy Spirit that are hidden in the puzzle below. The first letter of each word is given.

P	E	N	T	E	C	O	S	T
A	H	E	L	P	E	R	X	O
T	R	U	S	E	A	S	Y	N
I	O	O	P	A	W	I	N	G
E	A	R	L	C	I	H	U	U
N	O	W	G	E	N	T	L	E
T	H	E	I	R	D	R	L	S
R	O	O	F	I	R	E	E	W
E	A	T	T	G	U	I	D	E

P _____
H _____
G _____
F _____
G _____
P _____
G _____
P _____
W _____
T _____

REMEMBERING TO STOP and THINK!

Our bodies often show us and others how we are feeling. Look at each of the pictures below and find the clues that tell how the person is feeling. Draw a line from the word that describes a feeling to the face that matches the feeling.

HAPPY

ANGRY

EMBARRASSED

WORRIED

Sometimes our bodies give us clues about our feelings that others may not be able to see. These clues can remind us to stop and think before we react to people or situations. For example, when we feel anger, our heart might beat more rapidly, the palms of our hands might begin to sweat, or our stomach might feel tight. A good problem solver uses these clues as a reminder to stop and think before acting.

Have you ever had a time when you were feeling nervous and your stomach felt funny? We sometimes describe this feeling as "having butterflies in our stomach." This is something we feel on the inside. Nobody else would notice unless we told them how we felt. Can you remember the last time *you* had butterflies in your stomach? What do you think your body was trying to tell you?

Michael Forgets to Stop and Think

Michael and Maria are neighbors and friends. They play together almost every day after school. Sometimes they ride bikes. They often pretend they are explorers in outer space.

One day, Michael wanted to play soccer. Maria wanted to play a game of space explorers. "We *always* play explorers. Let's play soccer for a change!" Michael suggested. But Maria refused. "No way! It's explorers or nothing!" she said very loudly. Michael got mad and said to Maria, "You always have to have your way!" "That's not true!" Maria yelled. Michael yelled back to her, "It *is* true, and if you won't play soccer then I'm going home!" Michael called Maria a baby and stomped home.

Discuss

1. What is Michael's problem?

2. What is Michael's goal?

3. At what point in the story did Michael need to STOP and THINK?

4. How might the story have changed if Michael had remembered to STOP and THINK?

Following Jesus

Jesus calls us to be his friend and to be friends with one another. We may often disagree with others, but Jesus wants us to find helpful, not hurtful, ways to handle these disagreements. By remembering to STOP and THINK, we give ourselves more time to find the best solutions.

PRAYER

Jesus, I am sorry for the times I acted in ways that were unkind and hurtful to others. Help me to remember to stop and think each time I have a problem so that I may find solutions that are helpful, not hurtful. Thank you, Jesus. Amen.

OPENING DOORS
A Take-Home Magazine™

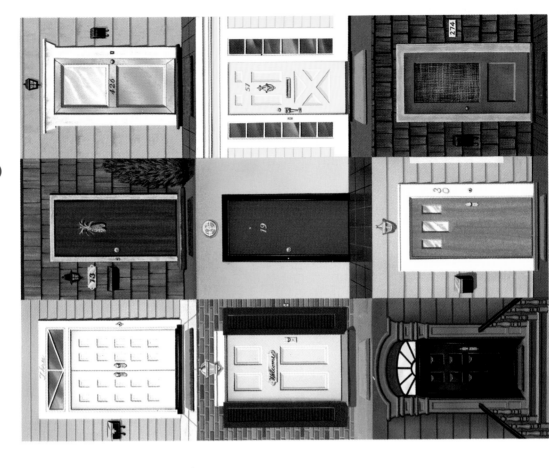

Growing Closer

COMPOSE A FAMILY CREED. Ask each person to write on a sheet of paper three things he or she believes in most. Then on a posterboard, print what each one believes under the words *We Believe*. Hang your family creed in a special place.

THINK ABOUT YOUR FAMILY'S FAITHFULNESS. How are you present to your family? Do you try to spend time together? Do you stay in touch with family members who live far away or are confined to their homes? Do you pray for one another? How can you better show your unending love for your family?

Looking Ahead

Unit 3 will help your child learn about the many ways we, as Catholics, worship. The unit will focus first on praying and on the many different kinds of prayer known and practiced by Catholics. Then your child will learn that the most unique characteristic of Catholic worship is the community celebration of the seven sacraments.

CLAIMING THE PROMISES OF BAPTISM

When adults were baptized in the early Christian communities of the first century, they were immersed three times. Each time, they were asked, "Do you believe?" With their first response of "yes," they were baptized in the name of the Father; with their second response, in the name of the Son; and with their third response, in the name of the Holy Spirit.

The baptismal questions beginning with "Do you believe" are used in the Easter Vigil and the Easter Sunday Mass in the Church today. The questions asked by the priest and our responses of "I do" form what we call the baptismal creed, or the Renewal of Baptismal Promises.

Each time we recite the creed, in any form, we make a statement of our faith, which began at our Baptism. The promises of Baptism are not only those that parents and godparents make to help a child live as a follower of Jesus. As significant as those promises are, one of the most noteworthy promises of the sacrament of Baptism is the promise of eternal life that *God* makes to the child or adult being baptized! Through our baptismal faith, which we affirm in our lives and in our worship, we *inherit* eternal life with God.

In the First Letter of Peter in the New Testament, we read that in Baptism, God "gave us a new birth to a living hope . . . to an inheritance . . . kept in heaven for you who by the power of God are safeguarded through faith" (1 Peter 1:3–5). A special practice used in the ceremony of Baptism for several centuries signified this blessing of Baptism. A drink of milk and honey was offered to newly baptized persons to remind them of God's promise to the Hebrew people in the

The **Apostles' Creed,** based on the teachings of the Apostles, also originated as a baptismal creed in the second century. The text of this creed first appeared in a handbook of Christian doctrine written in the eighth century. Today, it is used in Protestant liturgy and in the Roman Catholic rite. In the Roman rite, it is used specifically for the sacrament of Baptism and in Masses for children.

The Apostles' Creed describes Jesus as God's only Son and then recounts the events of his conception, birth, passion, death, resurrection, ascension, and second coming. The Nicene Creed, crucial in the fight against Arianism, includes a further description of Jesus that emphasizes his divinity.

In the shorter Apostles' Creed we say, "*I believe,*" which reminds us that faith comes from within the heart of each believer. In the Nicene Creed we say, "*We believe.*" This creed not only affirms the faith of our parish families but also joins these local faith communities together with the whole people of God who have shared a living tradition for nearly two thousand years!

desert that they would inherit "a land flowing with milk and honey" (Exodus 13:5). As people of God, the Church claims this same promise of salvation today.

John baptizing in the Jordan River

Like the Apostles' Creed and the Nicene Creed, the baptismal creed summarizes our belief that God is love. This love reaches out to all the people of God's creation, who are born of that love. It is revealed to us in the gift of the Incarnation and in the nearness of the Holy Spirit. Indeed, our God is faithful and lovingly fulfills all promises.

The Creeds

Each Sunday, Catholics recite the Nicene Creed at Mass. You may have memorized this creed, but how much do you really know about this statement of faith?

In the second and third centuries, adults preparing to join the Christian community were given a creed that summarized all that Christians believed. As the basis for their instruction, this creed was recited by the catechumens as their own profession of faith immediately before they were baptized. In the fourth century, the Church formalized this creed to make a statement against Arianism, a teaching that denied that Christ was divine. We have come to know this formal statement of Christian faith as the **Nicene Creed**, which developed from the Council of Nicaea (325 A.D.) and the First Council of Constantinople (381 A.D.). Today, this creed is a part of the eucharistic liturgy in all Catholic Churches.

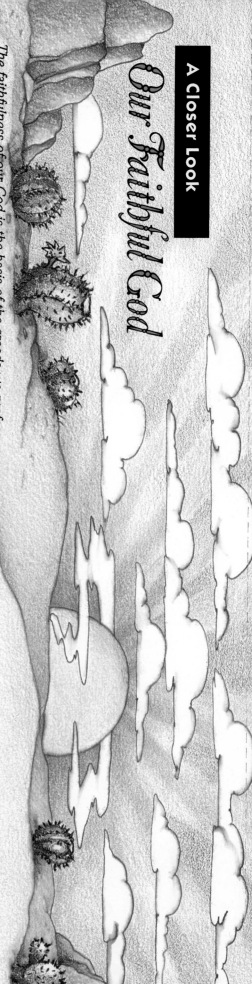

Our Faithful God

The faithfulness of our God is the basis of the creeds we profess as Catholic Christians. The Nicene Creed we say at Mass lists all of the basic beliefs of our faith. Read the pages of this magazine with your child. Enjoy the activity together.

What does it mean to be faithful? One of the best examples of faithfulness is the love our parents or guardians show us every day. No matter what we say or do, our parents continue to love us and provide for us.

At Mass we say the Nicene Creed. This creed, or statement of beliefs, reminds us of God's faithful love for us, the Church. When we recite the creed, we remember how God is always with us, day by day and year by year. We recall that God cares for us and has done many great things for us.

We believe that God has been faithful in times long ago. We know God's faithfulness to us now. We trust that God will be with us always, even until the end of time. We are proud to declare these beliefs together as members of the Catholic Church. We are grateful for God's loving care that will never end!

Identify all the true and false statements below. Then try to make the false statements true. Ask other members of your family to try them, too.

1. We believe in three Gods.

2. We believe in God's Son, Jesus, who lived, died, and rose to new life for us.

3. We believe that God did not send us a helper and guide.

4. We believe that the Church does not welcome most people.

5. We believe that we will live with Jesus forever.

When you go to Church, say the Nicene Creed aloud with the rest of the community. Think about what each part of the creed means to you. Thank God for being faithful!

UNIT 3

A Praying Community

What are some of your favorite times and places to talk to God?

Our Church Prays

Prayer

Sometimes when I am by myself,
I talk with God in prayer.
It feels so good inside to know
That God is always there.

God speaks to me in silence,
And that begins my prayer.
I know God always listens
To the thoughts I want to share.

I also pray with others,
Using words, and signs, and songs,
That help us celebrate the Church
To which we all belong.

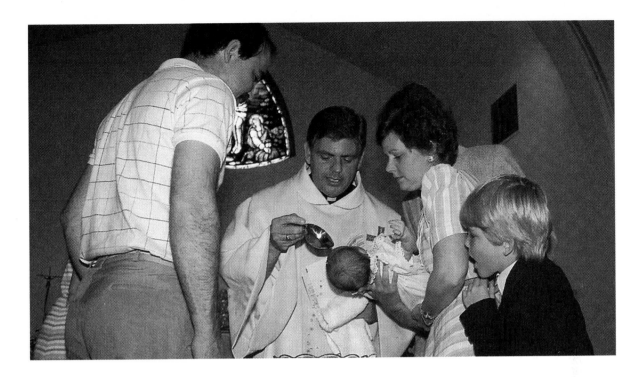

Many Ways to Pray

When we talk and listen to God, either alone or in a parish community, we are praying. Our **prayer** expresses our trust in God, as individuals and as a community of believers. Our words, our songs, and our gestures all help us to respond in faith to God's love for us. They are all part of our prayer.

We sometimes begin our prayer in silence. Sometimes when we are quiet, we can hear God speaking to us in our hearts. We sometimes pray like this in our parish churches before a Mass begins. God also speaks to us in the Scriptures we hear at Mass and when we read the Scriptures at home.

Each time we gather to celebrate the **sacraments**, we are praying in many ways. We listen to God's word and we talk to God in prayer. We know that the sacraments are special celebrations of Jesus' love for us and signs of his presence with us now. We hear about and experience Jesus' love and presence through the words, songs, and gestures of the celebrations. Can you think of some things you hear, say, or do at Mass that help you to know Jesus' love for you?

Vocabulary

prayer: listening and talking to God through our words, our songs, and our gestures

sacraments: special celebrations of the Church that show Jesus' love for us and are signs of his presence with us now

Jesus Prayed

Jesus prayed every morning, afternoon, and evening. Jesus also prayed at meals. He learned to pray at home from Mary and Joseph. They taught Jesus the **psalms**, the songs of prayer from the Old Testament. Mary, Joseph, and Jesus prayed as a family.

On Saturdays, Jesus went to the **synagogue** to pray with his family, friends, and neighbors. In Jerusalem, he liked to pray in the great Temple.

Jesus sometimes prayed when he was with crowds of people in busy towns. He also liked to go off by himself at times to pray in the hills and desert or along the shores of the Jordan River or the Sea of Galilee. Jesus experienced prayer as both talking to and listening to God.

His disciples noticed how much Jesus liked to pray. By his words and example, Jesus taught his disciples to pray as he did.

Based on many Gospel stories

Psalm Prayers

Some of Jesus' favorite prayers were the psalms. He prayed them alone and sang them with others. Here are some psalms you can learn by heart.

Of Faith
"O LORD, my God, in you I trust."

Psalm 25:1b–2a

Of Hope
"For you are my hope, O Lord."

Psalm 71:5a

Of Love
"I love you, O LORD, my strength."

Psalm 18:2

Of Petition
"O LORD, be my helper."

Psalm 30:11b

Of Thanksgiving
"I will give thanks to you, O LORD, with all my heart."

Psalm 9:2a

Of Sorrow
"Have mercy on me, O God, in your goodness."

Psalm 51:3a

Of Praise
"O LORD, my God, you are great and good!"

Based on Psalm 104:1b

Activity

The psalms show us how to pray to God in many ways. Write your own words for each kind of prayer in the box below.

My Prayer of Thanks _____

_____

My Prayer of Praise _____

_____

My Prayer of Sorrow _____

_____

My Prayer of Love _____

_____

Vocabulary

psalms: songs of prayer from the Old Testament

synagogue: a special place where Jewish people pray and study God's word

Activity

On a typical day, how many times do you stop to pray?_____

Think back to yesterday. What was happening? What were you feeling? Then write a short prayer for each of these times.

Morning Prayer: _____

_____

_____

Afternoon Prayer: _____

_____

_____

Evening Prayer: _____

_____

_____

_____

Christian Daily Prayer

Throughout the history of the Church, Christians have believed that praying often is important. The Scriptures tell us to "pray always, without stopping!" (based on 1 Thessalonians 5:17). Like the early Christians, some men and women in religious communities today continue the long tradition of praying together every morning and evening. Other Christians also gather together for prayer every day.

When we celebrate Mass in our parishes, we sometimes say we are celebrating **liturgy**, which means the official public prayers of the Church. The prayers that some Christians use to pray together every morning and evening are called the **Liturgy of the Hours**. These are also official public prayers of the Church. These prayers express our faith that God is with us always, from sunrise to sunset, every hour of the day. The Liturgy of the Hours includes singing or reading psalms from the Scriptures, reciting The Lord's Prayer, and praying petitions that express our concern for the needs of the Church.

Vocabulary

liturgy: the official public prayers of the Church

Liturgy of the Hours: the official prayers of the Church that some Christians pray together every morning and every evening

Prayer and Friendship

When we are good friends with someone, we usually spend time talking to them, listening to them, and playing with them. Whenever we can, we include them in our family activities and celebrations, too. The more time we spend with our friends, the closer we become.

On the other hand, we may have a friend who seems too busy to talk to us or to do things with us. When this happens, we may start to think that this friend does not want to be our friend anymore. This can make us feel angry or sad.

We know that God is always with us and that we can pray at any time. But it is only when we take the time to talk to and listen to God in prayer that we can say we have a friendship with God. The more often we pray, the more we show God that our friendship is very important. We can do this by spending some quiet time listening to God. God likes spending quiet time with us as much as hearing us pray aloud. When we do use words to pray, we can use prayers we have learned at Mass or in Religion class. Or we can use our own words. We can talk to God in the same way that we would talk to a close friend. When we are not sure what to say to God in prayer, we can just be still or we can ask the Holy Spirit to help us find the words to say.

We have learned that we can pray in many ways and at any hour of the day. The most important thing is to take the time to pray. The more time we spend in prayer, the closer our relationship with God can become. Whether we are praying alone, with our family, or with our parish community, we believe that prayer can bring us closer to God and to all those with whom we pray.

Activity

The sentences below describe some of the ways Catholics pray. For each sentence that describes a way that you have spent time with God, write an **X** on the line. For each sentence that describes a way to spend time with God that you will try sometime soon, write an **S** on the line. Then complete the last sentence to tell about one more way you can spend time with God. Be sure to try some new ways to pray sometime SOON!

_____ I listen to God in quiet before Mass begins.

_____ I talk to God early in the morning.

_____ I pray with my friends in Religion class.

_____ I say a prayer before I go to bed at night.

_____ I pray to God in my own words.

_____ God speaks to me through the Scriptures at Mass.

_____ I pray at meals with my family.

_____ God speaks to me when I read the Scriptures at home.

One more way that I can pray is _____

_____

_____

_____

_____.

We Believe

God calls believers to pray. The Scriptures tell many stories of Jesus praying, both alone and with others. Jesus gives us the Holy Spirit to help us pray.

Praying with the Psalms

Psalm 148 is often used in the Liturgy of the Hours for morning prayer. It is a psalm of praise for all that God has created. Before you begin this prayer, share with your class some of the wonders of creation for which you want to praise God.

The next time you pray in the morning, try to pray your own prayer of praise. Your voice will be heard by God along with the voices of many other Christians around the world who are praising God in the morning!

Leader: Look around the world!
See how many wonderful things there are!
LET THE HEAVENS AND THE EARTH PRAISE GOD!

All: LET THE HEAVENS AND THE EARTH PRAISE GOD!

Side 1: Even the sun and the moon join in praising God;
the shining stars adore the Lord of all creation!
Fire, rain, and wind are all in God's command.

Side 2: All the creatures of the sea and all birds of the sky,
all the animals of the earth, both wild and tame,
praise God!
Every living creature lifts up a song of praise!

All: LET THE HEAVENS AND THE EARTH PRAISE GOD!

Side 1: The mountains and the hills praise God,
the trees, the deserts, and the swamplands,
the seashores and all that is between them
praise the Lord!

Side 2: Let leaders and peoples from all nations praise God!
Let the young and the old, the women and the men,
families and loved ones all join in praising the Lord
of all creation!

All: LET THE HEAVENS AND THE EARTH PRAISE GOD!
AMEN!

Based on Psalm 148

Chapter Review

Write the code letter(s) that tells which type of prayer each psalm below is an example of.

> ### CODE
> PE = Prayer of Petition   F = Prayer of Faith
> T = Prayer of Thanksgiving
> S = Prayer of Sorrow   PR = Prayer of Praise

1. _____ "O LORD, my God, you are great and good!"

2. _____ "Have mercy on me, O God, in your goodness."

3. _____ "O LORD, be my helper."

4. _____ "O LORD, my God, in you I trust."

5. _____ "I will give thanks to you, O LORD, with all my heart."

Fill in the answers to the first two questions.

1. What is prayer? _____

_____

_____

2. What are some ways the Church prays? _____

_____

_____

_____

Pray often in the Spirit.
Based on Ephesians 6:18

3. Talk about some reasons prayer is so important in our relationship with God.

Our Church Celebrates Initiation

A Ceremony of Welcome

Many groups have special ways of preparing and welcoming new members. People who want to become members of certain groups go through an **initiation** that includes learning about the group and being welcomed into the group. New members are welcomed into the group in a special ceremony.

Initiation ceremonies usually use special *words* and special *actions*. They may also include special *signs* or *symbols* as well.

Look at the pictures above. What do you think is happening in each picture? How can you tell that the new members are being welcomed? What do the words, actions, and signs or symbols in the pictures tell you?

To what groups, clubs, or teams do you belong? What did you have to do to become a member?

Signs of Welcome at Church

When Jesus invites us to believe that he loves us and to follow in his ways, he calls us to live as members of the Christian community. The Church uses special words, symbols, and actions to welcome new members and to remind the people in parish communities that they belong to the family of Jesus' followers. The Church welcomes new members through the three sacraments of initiation: Baptism, Confirmation, and Eucharist.

In Baptism, we are united with Jesus and the Church and are welcomed into the Church for the first time. In Confirmation, the Holy Spirit helps us grow as Christians. And in the Eucharist, we deepen our unity with Jesus and with other Catholics in our parishes and around the world.

Discuss

1. What words, symbols, or actions would you use to welcome a new member to your family or a guest to your home?

2. What words, symbols, and actions help you to feel welcome in your parish?

3. What could you say about the sacraments of initiation that you have celebrated if you were talking to someone who is not a member of the Catholic Church?

Early Christian Initiation

Whenever the Church welcomes new members through the sacraments of initiation, we are reminded of who we are, who we are called to be, and how we have promised to live. In the Gospels, we read how Jesus teaches his followers to live. In the Acts of the Apostles and the letters of Paul, we read how the early Christians followed what Jesus taught.

Jesus told his apostles, "Baptize all people in the name of the Father, and of the Son, and of the Holy Spirit" (based on Matthew 28:19). And the apostles did just that. People who wanted to become Christians were baptized to show that they wanted to change their lives and follow Jesus.

"You will receive the gift of the Holy Spirit" (based on Acts 2:38c). The Acts of the Apostles is the book in the Bible where we learn about Pentecost and where we read about the apostolic Church.

"The bread we share is the body of Christ. The cup of wine we share is the blood of Christ" (based on 1 Corinthians 10:16–17). In his letters to the early Christian communities, Paul reminds them how important it is to share the body and blood of Christ. Today, the Mass is the most important prayer of the Catholic Christian community.

Activity

Write the answers on the lines provided.

1. In which sacrament today do people promise to live as Christians or to help their children live as Christians?

_____

2. In which sacrament today do we celebrate the gift of the Holy Spirit?

_____

3. In which sacrament do we share the body and blood of Christ as we remember what Jesus has done for us?

_____

Barbara's Big Day

It is the night before Easter. Barbara's parish is celebrating a very special Mass. Tonight, at the **Easter Vigil**, she will be initiated as a full member of the Church. Barbara is one of several people who will become a Catholic. Her family and friends are happy to be with her at the initiation celebration.

When she says the Apostles' Creed, her parents and godparents stand behind her.

The priest pours water on Barbara's head. He says, "I baptize you, Barbara, in the name of the Father, and of the Son, and of the Holy Spirit."

Her godparents give her a lighted candle. Her parents and godparents pray that Barbara will live according to the teachings and example of Jesus. Her friends join in that prayer.

The priest places his hands on Barbara's head. He prays that the Holy Spirit will be her helper and guide.

Then the priest confirms her. He makes the Sign of the Cross with oil on her forehead. He says, "Barbara, be sealed with the Gift of the Holy Spirit."

Barbara answers, "Amen."

The Mass continues. At Communion time, Barbara receives the Eucharist for the first time.

Later, the whole community has a party for Barbara. Everyone expresses their welcome and their love.

The Easter Vigil

As Barbara did, adults and older children often celebrate all three sacraments of initiation at the Easter Vigil. The Easter Vigil, the greatest feast of the Church year, is celebrated the night before Easter. At this Mass, the Church celebrates the resurrection of Jesus, the Light of the World, and his victory over darkness, sin, and death. We celebrate new life in Christ for both lifelong members of the Church and the new members who are being welcomed.

Vocabulary

Easter Vigil: the night before Easter, when the Church celebrates new life in Christ and the resurrection of Jesus, the Light of the World

Baptism: Yesterday and Today

In every Catholic Church, you will find a place where a person can be baptized. We call this place a **baptismal font** or a **baptismal pool**. Both the pool and the font contain water that is blessed and used to baptize. The pool usually has running water flowing into it. Often times, a priest may pour the water over the person's head. Barbara was baptized in this way. Sometimes, the person is baptized by **immersion**, which means the person's whole body is placed under water. In the early Church, people were usually baptized by immersion in a river or lake. A baby can be immersed in a large font or a pool. Adults and older children being baptized can stand or kneel

in a pool if the water is not deep enough for immersion. Does your parish have a baptismal font or a baptismal pool? Where in your church is it located?

Activity

Look at the two illustrations of Baptism on this page. Complete the chart below to indicate what is the same about the two illustrations and what is different.

Same: _____

_____

Different: _____

_____

Symbols of Initiation

When we celebrate the sacraments, we use many symbols to help us pray. Symbols help us to see the things we pray about or that we read about in the Scriptures.

In Baptism, water reminds us that we are celebrating new life. Water helps all living things to grow.

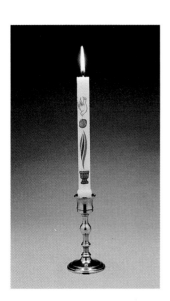

The light of the Paschal, or Easter, candle reminds us that Jesus is the Light of the World and that as Christians, we too can bring light to the world.

In both Baptism and Confirmation, we are anointed with oil to show that we have been chosen by God for a special way of life as followers of Jesus.

In the Eucharist, we receive the body and blood of Jesus to remind us of Jesus' love for us.

Vocabulary

baptismal font: a container for water that is used in Baptism

baptismal pool: a larger baptismal font in which a person can kneel, stand, or be immersed

immersion: baptizing a new Christian by placing his or her whole body under water

Praying a Rite of Christian Initiation

Reader: A reading from the Gospel of Mark (based on Mark 7:31–37). A man who could not hear and could not speak very well was brought to Jesus. The crowd begged Jesus to lay his hands on the man. Jesus took him away from the crowd and placed his fingers in the man's ears. Then he touched the man's tongue. Jesus looked up to heaven and said, "Ephphetha! Be opened." Immediately, the man could hear and speak clearly. When the crowd of people learned what had happened, they were very excited and told everyone about what Jesus had done. The gospel of the Lord.

All: Praise to you, Lord Jesus Christ.

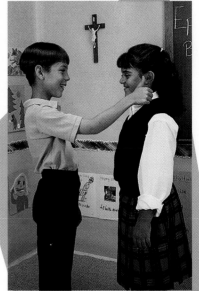

Leader: I now invite those of you chosen to be *Group 1* to turn to your partners. Make the Sign of the Cross on your partner's right ear, on the left ear, and on your partner's mouth. Say to your partner:

Group 1: Ephphetha! Be opened! Hear the word, believe it, and share it.

Leader: I now invite each of you in *Group 2* to make the Sign of the Cross on your partner's right ear, on the left ear, and on your partner's mouth. Say to your partner:

Group 2: Ephphetha! Be opened! Hear the word, believe it, and share it.

Leader: Let us pray.

All: Jesus, we thank you for inviting us to be members of your family, the Church. Thank you, too, for all the people who are preparing to join the Church. Help us to welcome them, love them, and grow with them as Catholics who are faithful to your word. Amen.

Chapter Review

For each phrase in Column 1, write the letter of the matching word(s) from Column 2.

Column 1

_____ container for water that is blessed and used to baptize

_____ helps all living things to grow

_____ baptizing someone by placing them under water

_____ welcoming new members into a group

_____ the sacraments of initiation

_____ symbol used to show that we have been chosen to follow Jesus

Column 2

a. Baptism, Confirmation, Eucharist

b. baptismal pool or font

c. initiation

d. oil

e. water

f. immersion

Fill in the answers to the first two questions.

1. What is the *Easter Vigil?* _____

_____

_____

2. What are the three sacraments of initiation

and their symbols? _____

_____

3. Talk about some of the ways you can show people that you are a Catholic.

You are now members of the household of God.
Based on Ephesians 2:19

Our Church Celebrates Healing

Activity

When you go to Mass, who are some of the people for whom you pray?

_____

Who are some of the people for whom the Church prays during Mass?

_____

_____

What have you said or done to help someone who is hurting to feel better?

Praying for Healing

When we go to Mass, we often pray for people who are sick or who have died. We also pray for people who are alone, sad, or lonely. And we pray that people can forgive one another and live together in peace. In all of these prayers, we ask for **healing**. Healing takes place through the actions, words, and prayers that help people who are hurting to become well. When healing takes place, people who have been hurt feel better, and people who need forgiveness are forgiven.

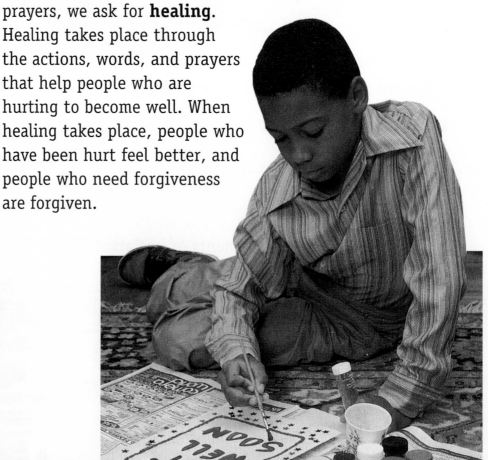

The Healing of the Sick Woman

One day, Jesus went to visit his friends Peter and Andrew. As Jesus arrived, Peter ran to Jesus. He said, "Jesus, my mother-in-law has a very high fever. Can you help her?"

Jesus went over to the woman. He took her hand and helped her to sit up. At once the fever went away.

The woman looked at Jesus and thanked him. Then she got up and prepared a meal for all the people who were there.

Based on Mark 1:29–31

Vocabulary

healing: the actions, words, and prayers that help people who are hurting to become well, to feel better, or to be forgiven

Anointing of the Sick

Ellie had been playing her radio very loudly again. Grandma screamed at her to turn it down. Grandma had been sick for a long time. Her pain was getting worse, and she was trying to get some rest. Ellie's father decided to ask Father Ezaki to come to bless Grandma and pray for her healing.

Father Ezaki began the **Anointing of the Sick** by saying, "Peace to this house and to all who live in it. Let us pray that the Lord will bring healing and peace to your grandmother."

Grandma asked Father Ezaki to take a moment to celebrate the sacrament of Reconciliation with her as well. Sometimes when people pray for physical healing, they also pray to be healed in other ways, such as being forgiven for any wrong they may have done. So Ellie and her father left the room. Grandma confessed that she had been yelling at Ellie. Grandma was sorry. She knew that she probably hurt Ellie's feelings. Father Ezaki suggested a penance. "Maybe you can give Ellie a kiss to let her know that you are sorry and that you really love her." Grandma asked God to forgive her. Father Ezaki absolved her in the name of Jesus and the Church.

Ellie and her father came back into the room. The Anointing of the Sick continued. Ellie's father read from one of the Gospels about Jesus' forgiving and healing a paralyzed man.

Then Father Ezaki placed his hands on Grandma's head. He prayed in silence for her to be healed. They all prayed that Grandma would become well and feel better.

Father Ezaki dipped his thumb in blessed oil and traced the Sign of the Cross on her forehead. He prayed, "Through this holy **anointing** may the Lord in his love and mercy help you with the grace of the Holy Spirit." He then traced the Sign of the Cross on her hands. "May the Lord who frees you from sin save you and raise you up," he prayed.

They all prayed The Lord's Prayer together. Ellie hugged her Grandma and told her how sorry she was for playing her music so loudly. Grandma hugged her back and said, "I'm very sorry I shouted at you. And don't ever forget how much I love you." Father Ezaki blessed them all. They were all grateful for God's gift of peace.

Two Sacraments of Healing

There are two special ways that Jesus heals our hurts, forgives us, and helps us make up with friends whom we've hurt. They are the Church's two sacraments of healing: Anointing of the Sick and Reconciliation. Sometimes they are celebrated together, but they are usually celebrated at different times.

Vocabulary

Anointing of the Sick: the sacrament of comfort and strength, of forgiveness, healing, and peace

anointing: putting blessed oil on a person's body as a sign of love, respect, or honor

We Believe

The Church brings Jesus' forgiveness and healing through the sacraments of healing. These sacraments are Anointing of the Sick and Reconciliation.

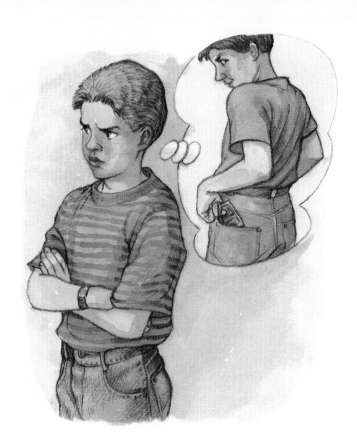

Seeking Forgiveness

One day after school, Derek and Marc were showing each other their baseball card collections. They both had several cards that were the same. Suddenly Marc remembered that his brother Steve had one special card that was very valuable. He decided to show it to Derek without asking Steve's permission.

Derek and Marc were both excited as they talked about the valuable card. When Marc's mother came home, she brought some freshly baked cookies and invited them into the kitchen.

Later, when Derek went home, Marc noticed that Steve's most valuable card was missing. He looked for it everywhere. Steve would be very angry. Finally, Marc called Derek and accused him of stealing the card. Derek said that he did not take it, but Marc was sure he had.

When Marc went to school the next day, he told his friends what had happened. No one spoke to Derek or invited him to visit for the rest of the week.

The next Saturday, when Marc came home for dinner after baseball practice, Marc's father said, "By the way, Marc, while we were cleaning today we found that baseball card you've been looking for. It was under the sofa in the living room."

Discuss

1. How do you think Marc felt when he discovered Steve's card was missing?

2. How do you think Derek felt when Marc accused him of taking the card?

3. What could Marc do, now that he found out what really happened?

Forgiveness and Sin

Sometimes we say or do something that we do not know will end up hurting someone. For example, you might borrow your older sister's drawing pencils without her permission. She may have been happy to let you use them before, but this time she gets angry. Other times we know that what we will say or do is wrong and may hurt someone, and we do it anyway. This is what we call a **sin**. Sin always hurts our relationship with another person and with God.

When we do something that is a sin, we can ask for forgiveness from God and anyone whom we have hurt. Seeking forgiveness is more than saying, "I'm sorry." When we ask for forgiveness, we are asking the person whom we have hurt to still love us or be our friend. Forgiveness is loving someone or being someone's friend even when they have hurt us on purpose. When we commit a sin, the sacrament of Reconciliation is a way to seek forgiveness from God. When someone has committed a sin that has hurt us, we can offer forgiveness to them.

Activity

Put a check in front of the situations below in which someone is hurting another person on purpose. Then talk about some ways he or she may want to ask for forgiveness.

_____ Breaking a window accidentally

_____ Telling lies about a friend or classmate, when you know what you are saying is not true

_____ Taking money out of your mother's wallet to buy something you want

_____ Calling people names

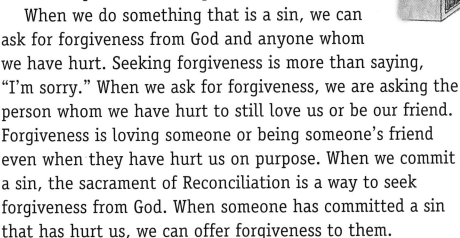

Vocabulary

sin: anything we do or say that we know is wrong and may hurt others and our relationship with God

Healing Our Hearts

We are called to accept God's healing and forgiveness and to bring healing and forgiveness to others. We are called to share God's peace. Before receiving the Eucharist, we all say, "Lord, I am not worthy to receive you, but only say the word and I shall be healed." What do you think this means?

When we hurt from sickness or sin, God does not forget us. Jesus reaches out to us. The Holy Spirit is with us. The Church gathers around us to comfort and forgive us.

The sacrament of Anointing of the Sick is for anyone who is sick and for those who are weakened in their old age. When the priest anoints us, it is Jesus Christ who strengthens us, heals us, and gives us peace.

The sacrament of Reconciliation celebrates God's forgiveness and our reconciliation with the Church community, whom the priest represents. When the priest absolves us, it is Jesus Christ who forgives us. Normally we celebrate the sacrament of Reconciliation by itself, but it may also be celebrated along with the Anointing of the Sick.

We Are All Healers

When God forgives us or makes us well, he is a healer. Each time we offer forgiveness to someone who has hurt us, we are healers. Each time we help take care of someone who is sick, we are healers. And each time we pray for someone to be healed or forgiven, we are healers.

Jesus calls us to love one another in all that we do and say. Sometimes this can be difficult. But we are called to forgive one another, be patient with one another, and be united with one another. So even when we Christians hurt one another, we can know the power of healing words and actions that show that we can continue to love one another and be friends.

Activity

Look at the people in the pictures. What could you do to help heal their hurts? Draw yourself doing something to help them.

Praying for Healing and Forgiveness

Leader: As we pray today, we remember how important it is to have faith that Jesus has the power to heal. In the Gospel stories about Jesus' healing and miracles, Jesus very often tells the person who has been healed that it is his or her faith that makes the healing possible. At Mass, just before the priest receives the Eucharist, we all say, "Lord, I am not worthy to receive you, but only say the word and I shall be healed." We can know the healing power of Jesus in the Eucharist, too. Today, you will be anointed with oil. As an expression of your faith in Jesus' power to heal, you can say "Amen," which means "I believe it is so." Let us pray.

Leader: Lord God, we thank you for your Son, Jesus Christ, who brings us healing and forgiveness. May your blessing be upon each of us now, as we are anointed with oil. In Jesus' name we pray.

All: Amen.

Leader: I invite you all to be anointed with this oil today. As you are anointed, know that Jesus is the great healer who can bring you comfort and strength when you are not well, forgiveness and peace when you have hurt someone. Receive Jesus' healing and forgiveness.

Leader: (The Leader anoints each student by making the Sign of the Cross on his or her forehead and says to each student:) Be well. Receive the peace of Jesus.

Student: Amen.

Chapter Review

Fill in the correct word(s) to complete each sentence. Then use the letters from the words you wrote to find the answer to the question below.

1. When a priest puts the blessed oil of the sick on someone's body, the priest is celebrating the sacrament of

   __A__ ___ ___ ___ ___ ___ ___ ___ ___ of the ___ ___ ___ ___.
   $\overline{1}$ $\overline{2}$

2. A __s__ ___ ___ is anything we say or do that we know is wrong and may
         $\overline{3}$
   hurt another person or God.

3. When we have sinned, we ask for God's forgiveness and peace in the sacrament of

   __R__ ___ ___ ___ ___ __c__ ___ ___ ___ ___ __t__ ___ ___ ___.
                                        $\overline{4}$

4. We know the __f__ ___ ___ ___ ___ ___ ___ __n__ ___ ___ ___ of
                              $\overline{5}$ $\overline{6}$

   God and others when they still love us even though we have hurt them on purpose.

What do we call the actions, words, and prayers that help people who are hurting to

become well, to feel better, or to be forgiven? __H__ ___ ___ ___ ___ ___
                                                     $\overline{6}$ $\overline{1}$ $\overline{4}$ $\overline{2}$ $\overline{3}$ $\overline{5}$

Fill in the answers to the first two questions.

1. What are the two sacraments of healing? _____

   _____

   _____

2. What does Jesus Christ do for us through the

   sacraments of healing? _____

   _____

God says,
"I, the LORD, am
your healer."
Exodus 15:26c

3. Talk about how we can be healers and peacemakers.

Our Church Celebrates Vocations

Activity

Each picture below shows someone doing something he or she enjoys. For each picture, talk about a career that you think this person might enjoy when he or she grows up.

What are three things that you do very well? Which of these do you enjoy the most?

How Christians Use Their Talents

In the Bible, we can read about our special talents and gifts. We can also learn how we are to use these gifts to help others.

"Each of us has received God's gifts. Some are apostles. Some are pastors and teachers. All are given gifts by God. These are to be used in ways of service to build up the body of Christ in love."

Based on Ephesians 4:7, 11–12, 16

"Put your gifts at the service of one another. The one who serves is to do it with the strength given by God."

Based on 1 Peter 4:10–11

"Whoever wants to be first must serve the needs of all."

Mark 10:44

Many People, Many Talents

Each of us has special abilities and talents. When we cherish and develop our talents, we enrich our lives and bring joy to others.

- Mary liked to write and draw. She became an artist. She met Luke, who was also an artist. They fell in love and were married. They now have three children. They help their parish by making special Mass booklets and bulletins.

- Gary is single. He always liked music. He learned to play the guitar and the piano and became a professional musician. He also gives free music lessons to children who want to learn to play but are unable to pay for lessons.

- Joan liked science. She also enjoyed taking care of people. She wanted to be like the Sisters who taught her. So Joan joined a special religious community of women. Sister Joan also became a nurse. She now cares for the sick in a country called Bolivia.

- Juan liked to read poetry and stories. Like Sister Joan, he felt a special need to serve God and to help people. So he became a priest. Father Juan likes to tell people stories about Jesus.

God Calls Us

When we are baptized, God calls us to live as Christians. Our parents and godparents promised to help us do this. God also has a specific purpose for each of our lives that makes us very special. God's call to cherish, develop, and use our own unique gifts for our own good and the good of others is known as a **vocation**.

There are vocations to many ways of living and of serving God. God calls some people to be parents. God calls some to be bishops, priests, or deacons. God calls others to be nuns, religious sisters, or brothers, who live in community with others who have the same calling, or vocation. God calls some people to marry and others to be single. All of these vocations are important.

Choosing a Vocation

As we grow up, we begin to recognize some of our own special gifts and talents. We can learn how to use some of our gifts to help others right now. At the same time, we also begin to think about what we will be when we grow up. When our parents, teachers, and other adults we admire live their vocations, they help us see the many choices we have. Someday, with God's help, we will choose our own vocation. We will make a promise, or a commitment, to answer God's call to use our talents for our own good and the good of others.

Vocabulary

vocation: God's call to develop and use our own unique gifts for our own good and the good of others

The Sacrament of Holy Orders

God calls some people to serve the Church as leaders in preaching God's word, in leading celebrations of the sacraments, and in helping others to live their own vocations. These leaders are called bishops, priests, and deacons. They are ordained in the sacrament of **Holy Orders** during a special Mass. Holy Orders is one of two vocations that the Church celebrates as a sacrament of commitment.

During the Mass of Ordination, the bishop places his hands on the head of each person being ordained. He prays that God will help them carry out their new roles. Those being ordained promise to spend their lives serving the Church as leaders and servants. The bishop then gives the newly ordained priests or deacons special signs of their service to the Church.

New bishops receive a ring, a shepherd's staff, and a stiff folded cap called a *miter*. New priests put on a special robe called a *chasuble* and a long strip of cloth called a *stole*. New deacons receive a stole and the *Book of Gospels*.

Religious Vocations

Throughout the history of the Church, many people have chosen to follow Jesus in a special way. Some have chosen the religious life of a priest, brother, or sister to help the Church spread the good news and grow in love.

Today, many parts of the world do not have enough priests and sisters or other leaders to help them. As Catholics, we need to pray for more people to dedicate their lives to continuing the work of Jesus in the world. Each year the Church sets aside a special Sunday as Vocations Awareness Sunday. On this day, we pray especially for vocations to the priesthood, sisterhood, and brotherhood.

We often learn about the possibilities for our own vocations from the good examples set by the priests, sisters, brothers, and lay leaders in our parishes and schools. Our families help us live the kind of life Jesus wants us to live so that someday we may also be open to the call to serve God in these same ways.

Activity

Complete the sentences below to tell about a leader in your parish Church or in the worldwide Catholic Church whom you admire.

A Catholic leader I admire is _____

_____.

I admire this person because _____

_____

_____

_____

_____

_____

_____.

Vocabulary

Holy Orders: the sacrament in which bishops, priests, and deacons are ordained to special service in the Church

We Believe

Everyone has a God-given vocation. All vocations are important. The Church celebrates two vocations with sacraments: Holy Orders and Matrimony. We call these sacraments of commitment.

Activity

Have you ever been invited to a wedding or seen one on TV? Maybe you have been a ring bearer or a flower girl in a wedding. What do you remember most about that special celebration? What symbols do you remember seeing that were part of this sacrament? Write down some of the things you remember about the last wedding you saw.

_____

_____

_____

The Sacrament of Matrimony

God calls some people to share their lives in marriage. The sacrament that celebrates the love and commitment between a man and a woman is called **Matrimony**. Like Holy Orders, it is also called a sacrament of commitment. Matrimony is usually celebrated at a Mass. The Bible readings and homily are about love and marriage.

The bride and groom promise to always love and care for each other, to always stand by each other, and to love each other in sickness and in health. They promise to welcome children lovingly and to bring them up according to the ways of Christ.

The bride and groom place a wedding ring on each other's fingers as a symbol of their love. The priest blesses them and prays that they will grow in their love and share it with others.

I Wonder

Inside myself I wonder,
What is it I will be?
My teachers and my parents say,
For now, I should be me.

Sometimes my *me*'s an artist,
Sometimes an Olympic star.
And sometimes a mechanic
Who fixes up a car.

Sometimes my *me* is single,
Sometimes a missionary.
And when I go to weddings,
I think that I will marry.

Inside myself I wonder,
What is it I will be?
Someday I will have grown to learn
What God has planned for me.

God Calls Me

Jesus promised that the Holy Spirit would help us in the decisions we make every day. The Holy Spirit will also guide each of us as we listen for God's special call. Some of us may receive the call to be priests, deacons, sisters, or brothers. Some may choose to marry and raise families or to remain single. Some of us will serve our parishes as professionals and others will serve as volunteers. When we pray for God's help—and take the time to listen in prayer as well—we can have faith that we are making good decisions and commitments to serve in the ways that God has planned for us.

Vocabulary

Matrimony: the sacrament that celebrates the lifelong and life-giving love between a man and a woman, who promise to love each other as husband and wife

Praying for Vocations

When we pray a litany, we sometimes use petitions to tell God our needs and concerns. A familiar example of this are the General Intercessions at Mass, which are sometimes called the Prayer of the Faithful. Today, we ask for God's blessing on people who have been faithful in the special commitments they have made.

Teacher: The Scriptures tell us, "There are different gifts but the same Spirit; there are different ministries but the same Lord; there are different works but the same God who produces them in everyone. The Spirit produces all these gifts and gives them to each of us according to God's plan" (based on 1 Corinthians 12:4–7). Let us pray.

Students: For all married couples, especially _____.

All: Lord, hear our prayer.

Students: For all people in religious communities, especially _____.

All: Lord, hear our prayer.

Students: For all Christians who choose the single life, especially

_____.

All: Lord, hear our prayer.

Students: For all priests, deacons, and bishops, especially

_____.

All: Lord, hear our prayer. Help us to listen and follow. Amen.

Chapter Review

Complete the sentences by filling in the blanks.

1. God's call to use our gifts according to his plan

   for each of us is called a _____ .

2. The two sacraments of commitment are _____

   and _____ .

3. When priests are ordained, they receive a chasuble and a _____ .

4. Newly ordained bishops receive a ring, a shepherd's staff, and a _____ .

5. Newly ordained deacons receive a stole and the _____ .

6. A symbol of everlasting love is the wedding _____ .

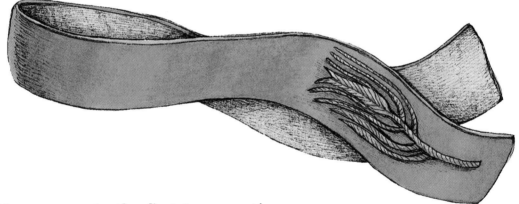

Fill in the answers to the first two questions.

1. What does *vocation* mean? _____

   _____

   _____

2. What are the two sacraments of commitment?

   _____

3. Talk about some ways a person can discover
   and respond to his or her vocation.

> **Live up to the calling you have received.**
> **Based on Ephesians 4:1**

UNIT **3** ORGANIZER

Prayer expresses our faith in God. In the *Prayer* box, write a sentence about the ways in which Catholics pray. Then for each of the *Initiation, Healing,* and *Commitment* boxes, write one thing the Church prays for in the sacraments. You may use any of the vocabulary words listed to complete this activity.

Prayer

prayer, psalms, synagogue, sacraments, liturgy, Liturgy of the Hours

_____

_____

_____

_____ .

Initiation

initiation, Easter Vigil, baptismal font, baptismal pool, immersion

The Church prays for

_____

_____

_____ .

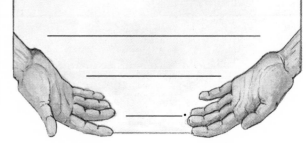

Healing

healing, Anointing of the Sick, anointing, sin

The Church prays for

_____

_____

_____ .

Vocation

vocation, Holy Orders, Matrimony

The Church prays for

_____

_____

_____ .

UNIT **3** REVIEW

Place an X before each true statement.

1. _____ God calls us to use our talents only for our own good.

2. _____ The sacrament of lifelong and life-giving love between a man and a woman is called Matrimony.

3. _____ The psalms are from the Old Testament.

4. _____ In Reconciliation, we celebrate God's forgiveness.

5. _____ Baptism is never celebrated at the Easter Vigil.

6. _____ Holy Orders is celebrated at a special Mass.

Fill in the blanks with the correct words.

forgives	synagogue	talents
followers	Temple	prayed

Jesus _____ every morning, afternoon, and evening. He prayed at home, in the _____, and in the great _____. As members of the Church, we are called to live as Jesus' friends and _____. Jesus _____ us when we hurt others. Jesus wants us to use the _____ that God gives us.

UNIT **3** REVIEW

Match the words in Column A with the definitions in Column B.

Column A

1. _____ psalms

2. _____ Holy Orders

3. _____ vocation

4. _____ prayer

5. _____ Liturgy of the Hours

6. _____ Easter Vigil

7. _____ sin

8. _____ initiation

9. _____ forgiveness

10. _____ healing

Column B

a. special celebration of the resurrection of Jesus and new life in Christ

b. the sacrament in which bishops, priests, and deacons are ordained

c. songs of prayer from the Old Testament

d. something that we know is wrong and hurtful to others and to our relationship with God

e. the ways we welcome new members into the Church

f. God's call to make a commitment to use our gifts and talents well

g. official prayers that some Christians pray every morning and evening

h. using words, songs, and gestures to listen or talk to God

i. helping people to become well or to be forgiven

j. loving someone even when they have hurt us on purpose

IDENTIFYING PROBLEM-SOLVING TERMS

Let's identify what we have learned about how Catholic Christians solve problems. Write the number for each term about solving problems next to the definition that best describes it.

1. Problem

2. Solution

3. Goal

4. Consequence

5. Stop and Think

_____ what the person with the problem wants to have happen

_____ a disagreement between people

_____ a way to solve a problem

_____ the first problem-solving step

_____ what happens as a result of a solution

Identifying Consequences

The game of tag has already started when Alice arrives outside for recess. Alice really wants to play, but the others say, "No, you're too late." Alice feels both sad and angry. She decides to stop and think of different ways to cope with the situation.

▼▼▼▼▼

Activity Choosing the Best Solution

For each possible solution, list some possible consequences. Then circle the best solution.

SOLUTION A	SOLUTION B	SOLUTION C
Alice could call members of the group names and tell them she doesn't really want to play anyway.	Alice could tell them she'll be "it" if they let her join.	Alice could ask some other kids who aren't playing tag if they would like to start a new game of tag.
Possible Consequences: _____ _____ _____	Possible Consequences: _____ _____ _____	Possible Consequences: _____ _____ _____

What Makes a Good Solution?

A good solution helps the person with a problem reach his or her goal. A good solution shows care for others. A good solution keeps a problem from getting worse. A good solution has positive consequences. A good solution shows Christian friendship.

Following Jesus

Jesus cares about us. Jesus knows that it is sometimes hard to figure out which solution is best. If our feelings have been hurt, we may find it difficult to choose solutions that treat others fairly and with kindness. Jesus gives us the Holy Spirit to help us choose solutions that show we care about others.

PRAYER

Jesus, I love you. Help me to solve my problems in ways that bring me closer to you, to others, and to truly living as a Christian. Thank you for giving me the Holy Spirit to help me choose what is good and loving. Amen.

OPENING DOORS

A Take-Home Magazine™

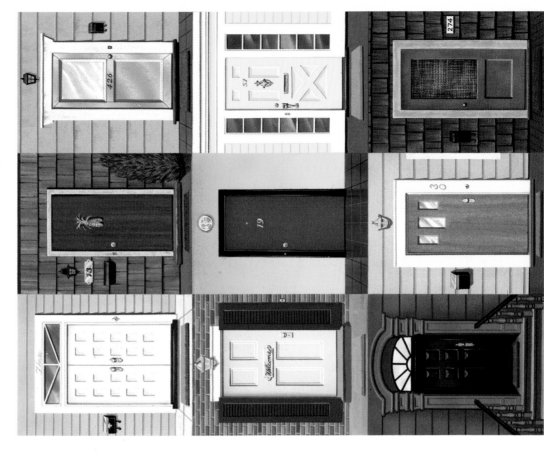

Growing Closer

WHO HAS TIME to pray? *You do* when you're...

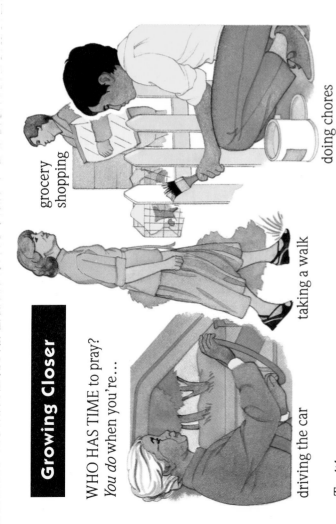

grocery shopping

taking a walk

driving the car

doing chores

Try it!

PRAYING MEMORIZED PRAYERS can be a good thing. These prayers provide prayer words when we cannot seem to pray in our own words. These memorized prayers also keep us united with other Catholics by allowing us to practice something we share in common. Write out the words of your favorite prayer and hang it in a place where you can see it—and pray it—often!

Looking Ahead

Unit 4 will center on the traditional moral principles of the Church. These principles find their roots in the life and teachings of Jesus, who drew upon the moral heritage contained in the Old Testament. Your child will learn that for Jesus and the Church, the basic law is that we love and care. Jesus and the Church stress that love of neighbor is the most basic sign of our love for God.

People of Prayer

Prayer is at the heart of Christian faith. And integral to Catholic life and faith is worship, or public prayer. Like Jesus, who worshiped in the Jewish temple, we value and pray the traditional prayers of our faith community. And like Jesus, who often went off to pray alone, we too are growing in our personal awareness of God's presence and activity in and through our lives. We believe that praying together supports the development of our prayerfulness as individuals.

The best and perhaps only way to learn to pray is by simply doing it. Growing up in a worshiping community, our children are learning to pray. Being in the presence of praying people, especially in our own families, and praying with them is the best way for our children to learn to pray.

A mong the more commonly known styles of black sacred song are the *spirituals.* Some spirituals that are becoming more and more familiar to American Catholic worshiping communities are "There Is a Balm in Gilead," "Let Us Break Bread Together," "Every Time I Feel the Spirit," and "Were You There." *European hymns* have been embellished with distinctively black rhythms and gestures. And a wealth of *new music* has been composed in recent years with the particular needs of the black faith community in mind.

B lack Catholic worshiping communities throughout the United States have been deeply affected by the introduction of black sacred music into Catholic liturgy, an introduction first attempted by Father Clarence Joseph Rivers in the late 1960s. For with black sacred song comes the artful use of music "to teach, comfort, inspire, persuade, convince, and motivate." It moves us to the depths of our being. It powerfully connects body and spirit, the sacred and the secular, the individual and the community.

A ll sacred music cultivates in us a deeper awareness of the presence of God. Black sacred music calls us to that awareness in a unique and engaging way.

An ancient insight in the Church is that *what we believe* is evident from *how we pray*. In other words, the way we worship reveals what we really believe as a community. In praying as individuals and as a parish community, we praise God, give thanks, express sorrow, and petition for specific needs. In all of this, we express our faith in our God who loves and sustains us.

By using familiar words and gestures and by designating a specific time and place for prayer, we can turn to God with great ease. Called to pray both together and alone, we take time to think about God, to talk to and listen to God, and to rest in God's presence. In all of our prayer experiences, we express and deepen the faith that calls us to live as one.

BLACK SACRED MUSIC

When we think about the sacred music most familiar to us, traditional songs such as "Now Thank We All Our God" and more modern songs such as "One Bread, One Body" may come to mind. In addition to these two styles of sacred song there is another type known as *black sacred music*.

Sister Thea Bowman, writing in the preface to the African American Catholic Hymnal *Lead Me, Guide Me* (G.I.A. Publications, Inc. 1987), tells us much about the origins of black sacred music, its unique characteristics, and its introduction into Catholic worship.

According to Sister Thea, "African men and women brought [to America] sacred songs and chants that reminded them of their homelands and that sustained them in separation and in captivity, songs to respond to all life situations, and the ability to create new songs to answer new needs." Sister goes on to tell us that "Black sacred song celebrates our God, His goodness, His promise, our faith and hope, our journey toward the promise." From the unique styles of African-American musical expression and a rich heritage of common stories and experiences, a new tradition of sacred song has emerged.

Prayers at Mass

Jesus taught us how important prayer is in our lives by showing us how important it was in his life. The Scriptures tell us that he sometimes went off to pray alone and that he also prayed in the temple. Spending time with God, telling God our needs, and listening to God speak to us is praying as Jesus prayed. Read the following with your child.

At Mass we pray together in many different ways. We pray together aloud and we pray together silently. We sing and sometimes dance. And sometimes the priest prays a prayer of the whole community and we answer, "Amen."

Some of the Mass prayers are listed here for you. Match each prayer line in Column 1 with a prayer line in Column 2 that is taken from the same Mass prayer.

1. … through Christ our Lord.
2. Our Father,
3. The Word of the Lord.
4. Let us give thanks to the Lord our God.
5. It will become for us the bread of life.
6. Christ has died,
7. Lamb of God, you take away the sins of the world:
8. We pray to the Lord:

A. who art in heaven…
B. have mercy on us.
C. Amen.
D. Thanks be to God.
E. Lord, hear our prayer.
F. It is right to give him thanks and praise.
G. Blessed be God for ever.
H. Christ is risen, Christ will come again.

Join in praying the many different kinds of prayers we pray at Mass. Remember to listen to God whenever you pray.

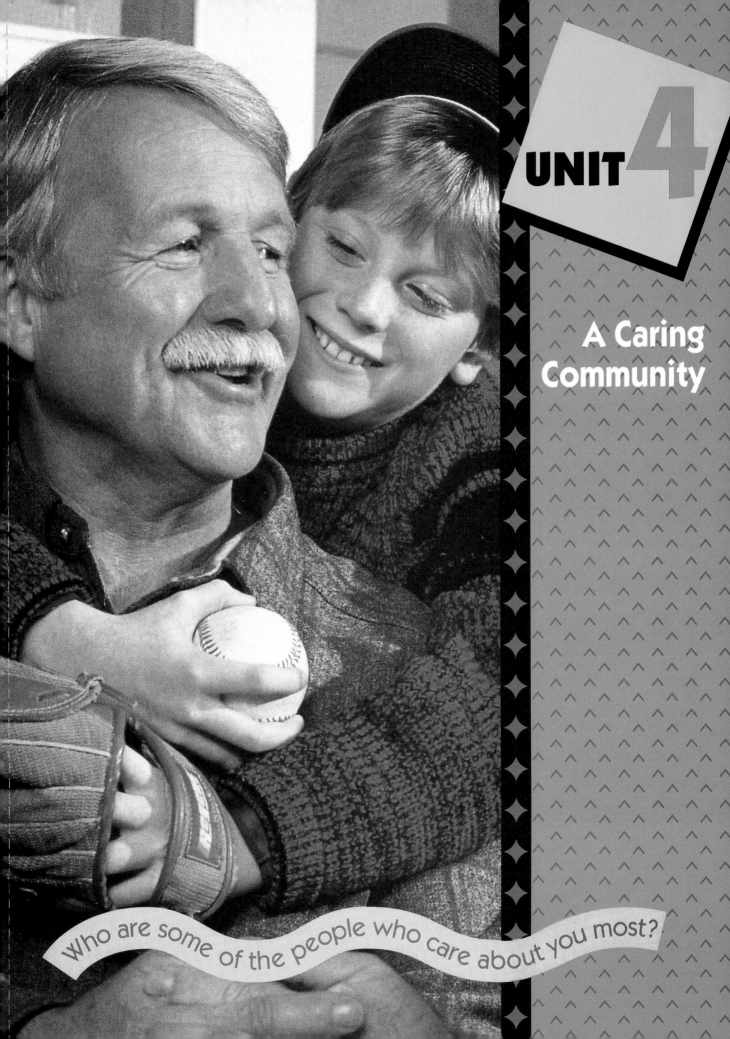

UNIT 4

A Caring Community

Who are some of the people who care about you most?

Our Church Teaches Us to Love

What are some good things about the rules that we live by at home, in school, in cities and towns? How do they help us and others?

To Call or Not to Call

Samantha loved talking to her friends on the telephone. Whenever the phone rang, she was the first to answer. She was always sure it was for her.

One day, Samantha's teacher sent a note home, telling Samantha's dad that she had not completed her homework for two weeks. Samantha and her dad agreed that taking away Samantha's phone privileges might help the situation. "If you even pick up that phone without asking, you'll be grounded for a month," her dad said. "And no playing outside after school!"

Samantha was sad, but she always obeyed her father. It was hard not to use the phone whenever she wanted. But she kept the rule for two days.

Then one afternoon when she was the only one inside the house, Samantha was looking out her window. The snow was falling. It was so pretty. The last thing Samantha wanted to do was her homework. She loved to daydream.

A few minutes passed. Suddenly, Samantha was startled. She saw her neighbor, Mrs. Green, slip and fall on the icy sidewalk. She couldn't get up. It looked as if her leg might be badly hurt.

Samantha ran to the front door of her house. Then she stopped. Samantha reached for the phone, then put it down. She thought of Dad's rules. Then she picked up the phone and dialed 911.

When Samantha's dad came home, she told him what happened. She expected her dad to be angry about her using the phone. To her surprise, he hugged her proudly and said, "You did the right thing."

Breaking the Sabbath Laws

One day, Jesus and some of his disciples were walking through a grainfield. The disciples were hungry and so began picking the grain to eat. Some **Pharisees** saw this and questioned Jesus about why the disciples were breaking the laws of the **Sabbath**, a day for rest and prayer. The Pharisees were very religious and based their entire lives on living according to God's laws. Jesus reminded them about a story from the Scriptures that tells about a time when David and his friends were also breaking the Sabbath laws.

Jesus left the grainfield and then entered a synagogue. He met a man there who had a broken hand. The Pharisees asked Jesus if it was lawful to cure this man on the Sabbath. Jesus asked them, "Would you not on the Sabbath lift out a sheep of yours that has fallen into a pit? And is not a human being more valuable than a sheep? Certainly, it is lawful to do good on the Sabbath."

Based on Matthew 12:1–12

Discuss

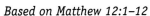

1. What did Samantha's dad mean when he told her that she did the right thing?

2. What did Jesus mean when he said "it is lawful to do good on the Sabbath"?

3. What might you have said or done in each story?

Vocabulary

Pharisees: very religious Jews who based their entire lives on living according to God's laws

Sabbath: a day for rest and prayer

◆ ◆ ◆ ◆ ◆ ◆ ◆ ◆ ◆ ◆ ◆

Jesus Teaches About Love 〜〜

One day, Jesus was talking to some well-educated men called **scribes**. One of them had been listening very carefully. He was impressed by what Jesus was saying. So he decided to ask Jesus a question.

"Which is the most important of all the **commandments**?" the scribe asked. Everyone listened to hear the answer.

"The first and greatest commandment of all is this," Jesus told them. "You shall love the Lord your God with all your heart, with all your soul, with all your mind, and with all your strength."

People in the crowd nodded their heads in agreement. Then they listened as Jesus continued.

"This is the second commandment," Jesus added. "You shall love your neighbor as yourself. There are no other commandments greater than these two."

The scribe was pleased with Jesus' answer. "You are right," said the scribe. "To love God with all our heart, with all our thoughts, and with all our strength, and to love our neighbor as ourselves is worth more than anything."

Based on Mark 12:28–33

Activity

Read the list below and place an **X** on the line before each sentence that tells one way that we can show our love for God and others.

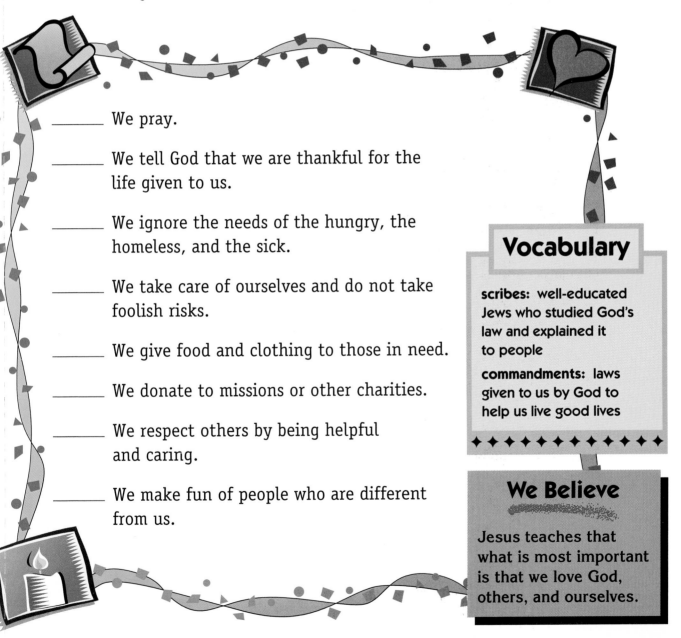

_____ We pray.

_____ We tell God that we are thankful for the life given to us.

_____ We ignore the needs of the hungry, the homeless, and the sick.

_____ We take care of ourselves and do not take foolish risks.

_____ We give food and clothing to those in need.

_____ We donate to missions or other charities.

_____ We respect others by being helpful and caring.

_____ We make fun of people who are different from us.

Vocabulary

scribes: well-educated Jews who studied God's law and explained it to people

commandments: laws given to us by God to help us live good lives

We Believe

Jesus teaches that what is most important is that we love God, others, and ourselves.

The Importance of Love

Love is very important to Jesus. When we read the Scriptures, we learn that Jesus often talks about whom we are to love and the ways we are to love. Jesus teaches us that it is especially important to love those whom it is difficult to love. These may be people who have hurt us in some way. Can you think of some of the people whom Jesus tells us to love?

Activity

Look up the following Scripture verses in your Bibles.

Whom does Jesus tell us to love?

Matthew 5:43–44 _____

John 13:34–35 _____

What else does Jesus say about the ways we can love others?

Matthew 5:43–44 _____

_____

Luke 6:27–31 _____

_____

_____

John 14:15 _____

_____

Activity

Next to each caption below, write the number of the teaching of Jesus that best fits.

1. Give to others generously; the greatest love you can show is to give up everything for your friends.

2. Pray for those who act mean toward you.

3. We can forgive those who hurt us.

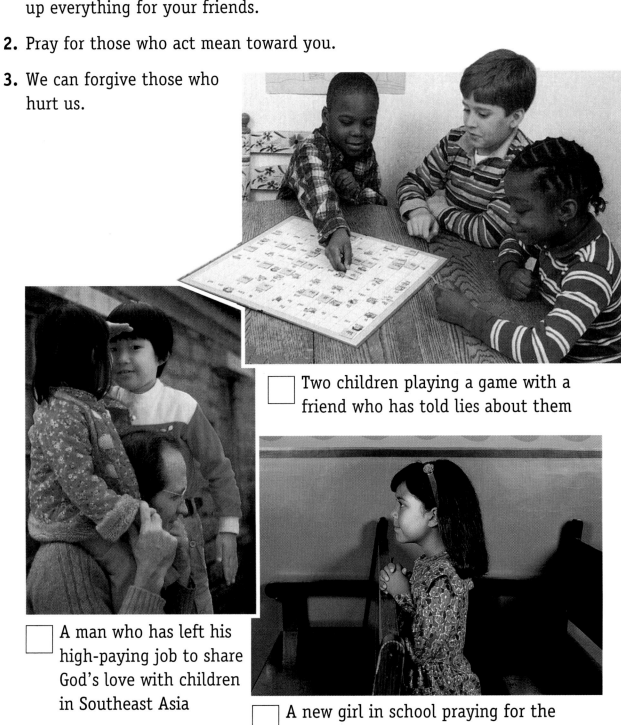

☐ Two children playing a game with a friend who has told lies about them

☐ A man who has left his high-paying job to share God's love with children in Southeast Asia

☐ A new girl in school praying for the students who make fun of her

Father Damien's Life of Love

We are called to show our love for God and for others every day of our lives. Some people show their love for God and for others in very special ways. They do all they can to reach out to love people who have nobody else to love them.

Father Damien knew about the people on Molokai, one of the islands of Hawaii. Molokai was a place where people who had a terrible skin disease called leprosy were sent.

Damien freely went to care for these suffering people, knowing he would probably get leprosy. For sixteen years he reached out to these people with love. He built houses for them. He taught them. He cared for children on the island who had no parents. He was doctor, nurse, priest, and friend to all the people on the island.

Eventually, Father Damien did get leprosy. He was sick for five years before he died in 1889. Damien lived a life of great love and service to God as he cared for these people who had nobody else to love them.

In 1995, during a visit to Belgium, where Father Damien was born, Pope John Paul II honored Father Damien by calling him Blessed Father Damien. He did this because Father Damien is a good example of a person who lived a very holy life and who suffered for the sake of helping others.

Giving Our All

There are many ways to show love for God and for others. Some of them are easy to do. But some things are hard to do. We are called to show our love for one another every day of our lives. We can love in big ways and in small ways. Every effort we make to show love is important to God. Like Damien, we can live a life of great love and service to God.

Activity

Underline the number of each action that shows love for God or for others. Circle the numbers of the things that are sometimes difficult for you to do.

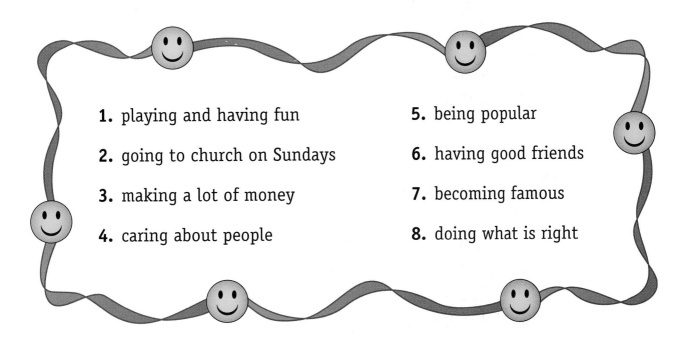

1. playing and having fun

2. going to church on Sundays

3. making a lot of money

4. caring about people

5. being popular

6. having good friends

7. becoming famous

8. doing what is right

Praying with Sign Language

Jesus teaches us that to love God and others is more important than anything. We have learned that prayer is one way we can show love for others. Prayer also shows our love for God. As we pray today, let us remember that all our prayers can be beautiful expressions of our love for God and for one another. Let us pray.

Leader: For all the times that you listen to our prayers,
All: We love you, God.

We   love   you,   God.

Leader: For loving us no matter what and for giving us Jesus to show us how great your love for us is,
All: We thank you, God.

We   thank you,   God.

Leader: As we learn to love everyone, even our enemies; as we learn to forgive those who have hurt us; and as we learn to love others as generously and completely as Jesus did, we pray,
All: Help us, God.

Help   us,   God.

Leader: God, we pray for those whom we find it most difficult to love. Help us always to remember that it is important to you that we find a way to love and forgive others. We pray all these things in Jesus' name.
All: Amen.

Chapter Review

| neighbor | Jesus | love | commandments |
| Pharisees | Damien | scribes | Sabbath |

Write the words that best complete the sentences in the paragraphs below.

In the choices that he made, _____ showed us that

_____ is more important than anything.

The _____ lived according to God's law. The laws of the

_____ helped Jewish people to set aside a day for rest and prayer.

The _____ studied and helped explain God's law to people. They

knew that the _____ were part of God's law. Jesus taught

that the two most important commandments were to love God and to love our

_____ as ourselves. Father _____ is a good

example of someone who loved God and others generously.

Fill in the answers to the first two questions.

1. What is a commandment? _____

2. What does Jesus say are the two greatest

   commandments? _____

   _____

3. Talk about what you can learn from Father
   Damien's example of love.

> **Let us love one another because love comes from God.**
> **Based on 1 John 4:7**

14

Our Church Teaches the Commandments

Obeying the Rules

There are many rules to follow in our schools. Our families have rules, too. These rules are important. When our teachers or parents teach us rules, they may tell us some good reasons to follow rules. We are sometimes told that rules are "for our own good." The people who set the rules are those who love us and those who have concern for our safety and well-being.

Do you always obey the rules at home and at school? Why or why not?

Activity

On the lines below, write two rules that you are expected to live by at home and two rules that you are expected to live by at school. Then tell the class why it is a good idea to obey each rule.

Home: _____

_____

School: _____

_____

Other Rules That Matter

We have learned about Jesus' commandment to love. We have learned that we should love God with our whole heart and mind and that we should love others as ourselves. These are the commandments that Jesus says are most important. He has told us this because he knows that when we obey these rules, we will be happy.

When Jesus talked about how important love is, some listeners thought that none of the other laws of God's people mattered anymore. One day, while Jesus was preaching on a hillside, he explained that *all* of God's laws are important. As a child, Jesus had learned many more of God's commandments. And when Jesus taught his followers, he often reminded them about these commandments and how important it is to obey them.

Words to Live By

For a long time, God's people have been guided by the Ten Commandments. Jews and Christians use these commandments as guides to living good and happy lives.

The Ten Commandments

1. I, the Lord, am your God. You shall not have other gods besides me.

2. You shall not take the name of the Lord, your God, in vain.

3. Remember to keep holy the Sabbath day.

4. Honor your father and mother.

5. You shall not kill.

6. You shall not commit adultery.

7. You shall not steal.

8. You shall not bear false witness against your neighbor.

9. You shall not covet your neighbor's wife.

10. You shall not covet anything that belongs to your neighbor.

Based on Exodus 20:2–17

Ways of Loving

God gave us the Ten Commandments to teach us how to love and care. The first three commandments show us ways to love God.

- We have faith in and trust God. God is the center of our lives. (1)

- We use God's name only with **reverence**. (2)

- We take time to pray, to celebrate the Eucharist, and to rest, especially on Sunday. (3)

The other seven commandments show us ways to love and care for others, ourselves, and the things that God has given us.

- We obey and respect our parents and others who take care of us. (4)

- We care for our health and treat others kindly. We don't hurt others. (5)

- We respect our own bodies and others' bodies. Husbands and wives love, respect, and are faithful to each other. (6 and 9)

- We do not steal or waste things. We are not greedy or careless. We do not cheat. We share what we have with others. (7 and 10)

- We always tell the truth. We are honest. (8)

Vocabulary

reverence: an attitude of respect, care, and honor

◆◆◆◆◆◆◆◆◆◆◆

We Believe

God gives us the Ten Commandments to help us live good and happy lives. The commandments show us ways of loving God, ourselves, other people, and all of creation.

Activity

We are called to lead good and happy lives by keeping God's laws. Read these four stories. Decide which commandment is being followed in each story. Write the number of the commandment in the box next to each story.

Caring About God

☐ It is a cold, rainy Sunday morning. Kim would like to stay in her warm bed, but she gets up and goes with her family to Sunday Mass.

Caring About Others

☐ Max is excited when Joe invites him to go fishing for the day. But then Max remembers that his parents had asked him to help Grandpa clean out his garage. So Max tells Joe he cannot go fishing this time.

Caring About Ourselves

☐ Carlos jumps on his bicycle and rushes to soccer practice. A block away from home, he stops, hesitates, and then rides back to get his helmet. He puts it on and then rides quickly to soccer practice.

Caring About Things

☐ Nicole did not do her homework. She watched TV instead. During recess, Nicole takes Emilie's math homework. She copies it and then slips it back into Emilie's desk. But during lunch, Nicole tears up the copied homework and does it herself.

Sally's Decision

On her way to school, Sally was thinking about a new video she wanted. Her birthday was still three months away, and she could hardly wait. Only a few blocks from home, Sally noticed a wallet lying on the sidewalk in front of her. She bent down, picked it up, and looked inside. She found pictures of a family from her neighborhood, along with some credit cards and $25 in cash. Sally looked around to see if anyone was watching. Then she decided to put the wallet into her backpack without saying a word to anyone. Sally continued on her way to school, still thinking about that new video.

Discuss

1. If you found a neighbor's wallet with money inside, what would you do?

2. If you stopped to think about the rules and commandments you have been taught, how might your response be different?

3. If Sally told you what she had done, what could you say to help her decide to return the wallet and the money?

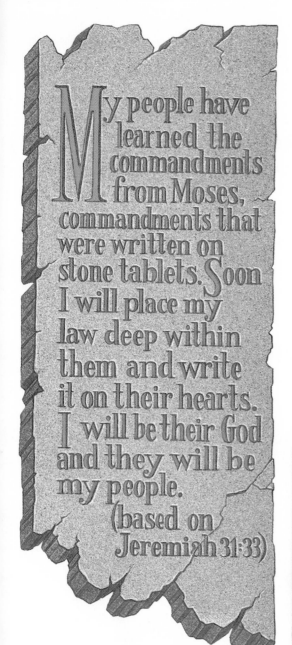

My people have learned the commandments from Moses, commandments that were written on stone tablets. Soon I will place my law deep within them and write it on their hearts. I will be their God and they will be my people.
(based on Jeremiah 31:33)

What Would *Jesus* Do or Say?

As Catholics, we are committed to living according to the rules that Jesus taught. If those rules ever seem difficult or confusing, we can recall stories from the Gospels to help us think about what Jesus would do or say in the same situation. We can even pray to Jesus, asking, "Jesus, what would *you* do?" or "What would *you* say if you were in my shoes, Jesus?"

When Jesus was a young child and made decisions, he may have taken time to think about God's commandments in the Scriptures. And he may have asked Mary or Joseph to guide him. But as he grew, he knew God's law so well that it became a part of everything he said and did. Jesus learned many things from the Scriptures.

When we know and understand God's law and believe that it is good, then we know that God's law is written on our hearts. And when we believe in the importance of love, as Jesus did, we pray for our hearts to be filled with love for God and others. We also pray that all the decisions we make will show that we are people of God.

Activity

As Catholics who are still growing in faith and love, we have many people and places to which we can turn for help as we make decisions.

For each question in Column A, write the number of the person or place from Column B that shows where you might find the answer to the question. A hint is given for the first one.

Column A

_____ Would Jesus use kinder words than this? (Hint: Where do we read stories about Jesus?)

_____ Is it okay to steal something I really want?

_____ Do I believe in my heart that this is right?

_____ Will eating too much of this make me sick?

_____ What rules can help make the playground safe for everyone?

Column B

1. mother or father

2. the commandments

3. teachers

4. the Gospels

5. myself

Praying with Scripture

When God gave the commandments, God's people agreed to live by them. And Jesus promised that whoever obeys and teaches these commandments will be called greatest in the kingdom of heaven. Today we pray for God's guidance and grace as we promise to be obedient to the commandments. Let us pray.

Leader: Lord God, your laws show us the way of Jesus' love. You have promised much happiness to all those who keep your commandments. Hear our promises today to live as Catholics who are faithful and obedient to the ways that lead to eternal happiness.

All: We will do as the Lord has told us.

Leader: Lord, you teach us to love and respect you, to place our trust completely in you, and to take time to pray.

All: We will do as the Lord has told us.

Leader: Lord, you teach us to love and respect our parents, to do our best to stay healthy and safe, and to treat others kindly.

All: We will do as the Lord has told us.

Leader: Lord, you teach us to respect and care for our bodies.

All: We will do as the Lord has told us.

Leader: Lord, you teach us to be responsible, fair, and honest in all that we do and say.

All: We will do as the Lord has told us.

Leader: Gracious God, we thank you for your gift of eternal life. And we thank you for being with us each day as your law grows deeper and deeper within our hearts. We pray in the name of Jesus Christ, our Lord, who leads us in the way of love.

All: Amen.

Chapter Review

Next to each phrase below, write the letter **G** if the phrase mostly shows a way to love God. Write the letter **O** if the phrase mostly shows a way to love and care for others, for ourselves, and for all the gifts that God has given us.

_____ Saying God's name with respect

_____ Telling our parents the truth

_____ Playing safely

_____ Trusting God to help us

_____ Being careful not to be wasteful

_____ Obeying our parents

_____ Taking time to pray, especially on Sunday

_____ Speaking kindly about our neighbors

_____ Making peace with people who would rather fight us

_____ Being grateful for what we have and not being jealous of what someone else has

Fill in the answers to the first two questions.

1. What is the meaning of *reverence*? _____

_____

2. What do the Ten Commandments help us to do?

_____

_____

3. Talk about how you can live according to the Ten Commandments each day.

> **Love one another by living according to the commandments.**
> Based on 2 John 1:5–6

Christians Help Others

Write a Dialogue

Write your own words in the story below to tell what you think the children are thinking or saying.

Who are some of the people you help and care for?

The Good Samaritan

Jesus taught many people during his lifetime. He often spoke to them in **parables**, which were brief stories that helped them understand what he was teaching. He once told a parable about a man who helped another man who had been beaten up and left for dead. Read the parable of the Good Samaritan in Luke 10:29–37.

Activity

Write the numbers 1 through 7 on the lines below to show the correct sequence of events in the parable of the Good Samaritan. The first one is done for you.

_____ The robbers left the man, whom they thought was probably dead.

_____ After bandaging the injured man's sores, the Samaritan took him to an inn.

_____ Later, a priest who was walking on the same road saw the man and crossed to the other side of the road to continue his own journey to Jericho.

__1__ After Jesus taught about loving our neighbor as our ourselves, a lawyer asked Jesus, "Who is my neighbor?" Jesus began to tell the story about a man who was beaten and robbed while walking along the road from Jerusalem to Jericho.

_____ The next day, the Samaritan paid the innkeeper and told him that he would pay for anything more the man needed.

_____ A Levite also saw the man and passed him by on the opposite side of the road.

_____ A Samaritan stopped when he saw the man and knelt down to see if he could help.

Vocabulary

parables: brief stories that helped people understand what Jesus taught

◆ ◆ ◆ ◆ ◆ ◆ ◆ ◆ ◆ ◆ ◆ ◆ ◆

For Those Who Care 〜〜〜

One day, Jesus was talking to a group of people. He told them how he would reward those who cared about others.

"To those people I will say, 'Come into my Father's house. You will be happy forever because when I was hungry, you gave me food. When I was thirsty, you gave me a drink. When I was a stranger, you welcomed me. When I had nothing to wear, you gave me some clothes. When I was sick, you cared for me. When I was in prison, you came to visit me.'"

"Then the people will ask me, 'Lord, when did we see you hungry and feed you? When did we see you thirsty and give you drink? When did we welcome you as a stranger or clothe you? And when did we visit you when you were sick or in prison?'"

"And I will answer, 'As often as you did those things for one of the least of my brothers or sisters, you did them for me.'"

Based on Matthew 25:34–40

Caring for Others

Jesus teaches us that when we care for or help people in need, we do it for him. We are asked to see Jesus' face in the face of each person we meet. The Church helps us remember what we are called to do for Jesus through people who are in need. We call these caring actions the **corporal** works of **mercy**. These actions are specific ways that we can help people who have physical needs. As followers of Jesus, we are called to bring the love of Jesus to all people and to love and care for each person as Jesus would. For just as we see Jesus in others, others can also see Jesus in us when we help them and care for them.

Vocabulary

corporal: affecting our bodies and the needs of our bodies

mercy: loving care or compassion

✦ ✦ ✦ ✦ ✦ ✦ ✦ ✦ ✦ ✦ ✦ ✦

Corporal Works of Mercy

1. Feed the hungry.
2. Give drink to the thirsty.
3. Clothe the naked.
4. Visit those in prison.
5. Shelter the homeless.
6. Visit the sick.
7. Bury the dead.

We Believe

We best show our love for Jesus when we help people in need. Jesus teaches that whatever we do for people in need, we do for him. Catholics identify the corporal works of mercy as seven ways we can care for people in need.

Activity

God cares for each of us. We should also care for one another. Showing that you care about others is the same as showing that you love Jesus.

Follow the maze on the hiking trip below to find a special message from Jesus about caring for one another.

Whenever _____ _____ _____ cared for one of _____ _____ sisters

or _____ _____ _____ _____ _____ _____ _____ _____ , you

_____ _____ _____ _____ _____ for _____ _____ .

Based on Matthew 25:40

Jesus' Works of Mercy

In the Gospel of Mark, we can read many stories about Jesus performing works of mercy. In Mark 1:40–45, we read about Jesus healing a leper. In this story, the leper is told by Jesus not to tell anyone that he has cured the man. But the leper is so excited that he tells everyone he sees. Then so many people want Jesus to help them that they come to him from everywhere. And even when Jesus tries to find quiet places to pray, people find him and ask for his help.

In Mark 2:1–12, we read about how Jesus heals a paralyzed man. The crowds that come to the house where Jesus is preaching are so large that nobody can even get near the door. The four men who bring the paralyzed man to Jesus have to open up the roof to get inside. They lower the mat that the man is lying on through the roof, right above Jesus. Amazed by their faith, Jesus heals the man while everyone watches.

People came to Jesus again and again because they believed he could do great things for them. In Mark 6:34–44, we read that Jesus feeds five thousand hungry people with only five loaves of bread and two fish. In Mark 7:31–37, Jesus heals a deaf person. And in Mark 8:22–26, Jesus heals a blind person.

Christians today may not be able to heal the sick as Jesus did, but they can help the sick by visiting them. Christians today may not be able to feed five thousand hungry people with only five loaves of bread and two fish, but they can share food with those who have little or none. Jesus calls Christians today to work together to help others in many ways.

Making a Big Difference

We are called to show our love for Jesus by doing good works for people who are hurting and in need. We are called to live the corporal works of mercy. Dorothy Day faithfully did just that!

Dorothy grew up in a large, happy family. She lived in Chicago with her mother, her father, and eight brothers and sisters.

Dorothy loved to read. But she was sad when she read about people who were poor and hungry. She was even sadder when she saw people who had worn-out clothes or little food, lived in broken-down houses and apartment buildings, and were out of work.

Dorothy became a newspaper reporter. She wrote about the poor. With a friend named Peter Maurin, she started a newspaper called *The Catholic Worker*. The two hoped their paper would bring help for the poor.

But Dorothy Day wanted to do even more. She saw people in New York City who needed food, clothes, and a place to sleep. She and Peter opened a house where these people could come for food, clothing, and shelter. Dorothy spent the rest of her life living with the poor and helping them in every way she could.

Dorothy Day died in 1980. She had truly lived the corporal works of mercy. Some people who saw and experienced what Dorothy was doing for the poor started Catholic Worker houses in other towns and cities. Dorothy Day planted a seed. Catholic Worker volunteers have helped that seed grow. They are making a difference as they continue to serve the poor today.

In Simple Ways

Like Dorothy Day, some Christians live the corporal works of mercy in extraordinary ways. Others live them in very simple ways. Jesus calls each of us to live the works of mercy in our own ways, wherever we are. We can do this at home, at school, at work, or at play.

Some of us may see people in need every day. Some of us may only read or hear about people in need. We can *all* take more time to look and listen for opportunities to help others. People sometimes will come to us for help. Sometimes people find it difficult to ask for help.

Activity

Think about some people in need. These can be individuals or entire countries. Perhaps you know these people or you have heard about them on the news. On the lines below, write about one thing you saw, heard, or read. Then describe one thing you can do to help the person or group that needs help.

What I saw, heard, or read: _____

_____

_____

_____

_____

What I can do: _____

_____

_____

_____

_____

Praying with Today's Headlines

In Galatians 6:2, Paul tells the early Christians that they are to help carry one another's burdens. A *burden* is something that weighs us down. The corporal works of mercy help us identify some of the burdens that many people experience.

Today, we will offer prayers of petition for the needs we identify from current newspapers or magazines. We will begin each petition by saying the name of the person or group for whom we are praying. Then we will include some action that can help that person or group. We will conclude each petition by responding together, "Help us to carry one another's burdens." One example is given for you.

Petition: For the families who were left homeless after last week's hurricane, that our government, our churches, and all of us will be generous in providing food, clothing, and shelter to them for as long as they need our help.

Response: Help us to carry one another's burdens.

Chapter Review

Find words from the chapter to complete the sentences below.

1. Jesus told _____ to help people understand what he was teaching.

2. The good _____ was the only one who stopped on the road to Jericho to help the injured man.

3. The Church gives us the _____ works of mercy to teach us some of the ways we can help others.

4. We best show our love for _____ when we help people in need.

5. In the _____ of Mark, we read many stories about Jesus' helping people.

6. _____ made a big difference for many people when she began the first Catholic Worker house.

7. One way we can help to carry another's _____ is to pray for one another.

Fill in the answers to the first two questions.

1. What is the meaning of *corporal*? _____

_____

2. What do the corporal works of mercy teach us?

_____

_____

3. Talk about some reasons the corporal works of mercy are so important.

Help carry one another's burdens.
Based on Galatians 6:2

16

Christians Comfort Others

Redfeather's Response

In school, everyone called him Matthew. At home, on the reservation, his real name was Redfeather.

Redfeather's first months in the new school were hard. He was shy. His classmates made fun of him. They laughed at him when he spoke because he always spoke very softly and politely.

Redfeather often ate alone. He spent his free time drawing in a notebook he never showed to anyone. One day, Joe and Gerry took the small notebook from Redfeather's backpack during recess. They wanted to see what was in it.

When they opened it they were amazed. On page after page were beautiful drawings of hawks, eagles, rabbits, wolves, horses, rolling hills, houses, and people. There were several drawings of Redfeather's grandfather.

Gerry and Joe felt guilty. So during lunch they slipped the notebook back in Redfeather's backpack. They did not know that he saw them. Redfeather felt hurt and angry.

The next day they asked Redfeather to draw a hawk for them. They were making a poster for their soccer team, the Hawks. Redfeather did not say or do anything right away. He was not sure how to respond.

Tell about a time when someone hurt you and you forgave them or a time when someone was annoying you and you were patient with them.

The Unforgiving Servant

Peter asked Jesus, "How often do you expect me to forgive someone who has hurt me? Should I forgive him seven times?"

Jesus said to Peter, "You need to forgive him seventy-seven times. Let me tell you a story to help you understand what I am teaching about forgiveness.

"A king wished to settle his accounts with his servants. The first servant, who owed the king a very large sum of money, could not pay. So the king ordered that the servant, his family, and all that he owned, be sold to pay the debt. The servant fell down on his knees and begged the king to be patient with him. 'Please give me more time. I will pay you back in full.' The king felt sorry for the servant and so released him and forgave his debt.

"Later, this same servant met another servant who owed money to him. He demanded that he be paid. The other servant begged for his debtor to be patient. 'Please give me more time. I will pay you back in full.' But the servant who could not pay his debt was thrown in jail. Others who saw what had happened told the king. The king was very angry that the first servant did not show the same compassion that had been shown to him. So the king had the first servant, who showed no mercy to his fellow servant, thrown into jail."

Based on Matthew 18:21–35

Discuss

1. Do you think the king's decision to be patient and forgive the first servant was a good one? Why or why not?

2. Why do you think the first servant would not forgive the second servant?

3. Why did the people and the king become angry?

More Ways to Help

The corporal works of mercy that we learned about in Chapter 15 are all important ways to help others. But we can help others by caring for them and comforting them in many other ways, too. In the story about Redfeather and in the parable of the Unforgiving Servant, the people who needed help did not need food or clothing. And they were not sick or in prison.

Redfeather's feelings were hurt. He needed *comfort*. He also needed *advice* about how to respond to Gerry and Joe. He wanted to make a *good choice* about *forgiving* them.

The first servant needed the *forgiveness* and *patience* of his king. And he could have used some *advice* about how to respond to the other servant who asked for his *forgiveness* and *patience*.

By describing some specific ways in which we can be caring, the Church helps us remember Jesus' example and teachings of the many ways we can show love. These ways of helping people and caring for them are called the **spiritual** works of mercy. These works of mercy help others in very important ways, too.

Spiritual Works of Mercy

1. Help others make good choices.

2. Teach those who lack knowledge.

3. Give advice to those who are confused.

4. Comfort those who are hurting.

5. Be patient with others.

6. Forgive injuries.

7. Pray for the living and the dead.

Activity

Sometimes we can show concern by talking with others. Complete the sentences using the words below. Then talk about the spiritual work of mercy that each sentence shows.

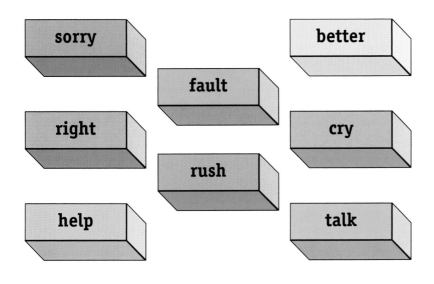

1. That's okay! It wasn't your _____.

2. Can I _____ you figure it out?

3. I'm _____ that you feel lonely.

4. I don't mean to _____ you. Take your time.

5. It's okay to _____. We are praying for you and your family.

6. I believe you are certainly doing the

   _____ thing.

7. I think you should _____ to your Mom about this, too.

Vocabulary

spiritual: affecting the mind, heart, or spirit

◆ ◆ ◆ ◆ ◆ ◆ ◆ ◆ ◆ ◆ ◆ ◆

Jesus Forgives Peter

Soon after his resurrection, Jesus had a special conversation with Peter. As they walked along the water's edge, Jesus asked, "Do you love me, Peter?"

Peter answered, "Yes, Lord, you know that I love you."

They walked in silence together until Jesus asked again, "Peter, do you love me?"

Peter must have been puzzled. "Why is Jesus asking me again?" Peter wondered. But he answered, "Yes, Lord, you know I love you."

As Jesus was questioning him, Peter must have remembered how, after Jesus was arrested, he had three times denied being a friend of Jesus. He had been afraid of being hurt by Jesus' enemies. "Now Jesus is giving me another chance," Peter thought to himself.

In a moment, Jesus asked him a third time, "Do you love me?"

Peter answered, "Lord, you know everything. You know well that I love you."

"Then feed my sheep," Jesus said to him.

Based on John 21:15–17

Encouraging Others

Peter knew that Jesus forgave him for the weakness and fear that led Peter to pretend he didn't know Jesus. Now Jesus was telling Peter to support, forgive, and encourage others. This is what Jesus meant when he said, "Feed my sheep."

Whenever we help and care for one another by performing any of the spiritual works of mercy, we encourage others. When we do not take time to comfort someone whose feelings have been hurt or to perform whatever work of mercy may be needed, that person may think that nobody cares. We all need to do our part to show that Catholics are caring and loving people.

Activity

Place an **X** before each sentence that says something a caring and loving Catholic might say.

_____ "Don't bother me! You should be able to do that on your own by now!"

_____ "We're all here for you. How can we help?"

_____ "It's okay. I know you didn't mean to hurt her."

_____ "I really don't have time to listen. I have enough problems of my own."

_____ "I know someone who can help you make the right decision."

We Believe

Jesus teaches us by word and example to care for people who are unhappy, who have problems, or who need help. In the spiritual works of mercy, the Church tells us some ways we can show care and concern.

Spiritual Helpers

We are called to forgive, comfort, encourage, support, and pray for others. We can follow the example of people like Angela Merici. Angela Merici, a saint, is someone who lived the spiritual works of mercy in an interesting and unique way.

As a young girl, Angela reached out to people who were hurting inside. Her father, mother, and sister died when Angela was very young. She knew what it felt like to be sad and lonely. This helped her care for others.

Angela loved children. Many of the children in her village in Italy were very poor. She wanted them to know about Jesus and the Church. She spent much of her time teaching them and taking care of them. She also brought comfort and hope to their families.

Many young women were inspired by Angela and her good works. They wanted to join her and help her with her work. So she organized them into a community of sisters called the Ursulines. They spent their time praying and helping people.

The Ursulines were the first community of sisters formed to teach young girls. The sisters still teach. They also spend their lives caring for people and helping them by living all the spiritual and corporal works of mercy.

Activity

Write a thank-you letter to a student in your class, to someone on your school's staff, or to a family member. Thank the person for showing you how their performing a spiritual work of mercy has made a big difference to you.

Spiritual work of mercy performed: _____

_____

Dear   ,

Praying in Our Own Words

Today, we will each thank God for someone who has encouraged us to live as faithful Catholics. The person may be someone who has helped us make a good decision or someone who has helped us understand something better. It may be someone who has given us advice or has comforted us. It may be someone who has shown us patience or forgiveness. It may be someone who has prayed with us. Maybe someone right here in our classroom has performed one of these spiritual works of mercy in our lives.

God, we thank you for the love and encouragement that our friends and families give us. Help us to be ready and willing always to encourage anyone who needs our help or our prayers. Amen.

Chapter Review

Choose words or actions from the "billboard" below that will help you along the road to becoming a loving and caring Christian. Write the words on the road.

Write the answers to the first two questions.

1. What does *spiritual* mean? _____

2. Name the spiritual works of mercy. _____

_____

_____

_____

> **Cheer the fainthearted; support the weak; be patient toward all.**
> **Based on 1 Thessalonians 5:14**

3. Talk about what your life would be like without people who live out the spiritual works of mercy.

In each heart below, write one thing you remember from the chapter and one caring action you will take because of what you learned.

Our Church
teaches us to love

Our Church teaches us
the Commandments

Christians comfort others

Christians help others

UNIT **4** REVIEW

Place an X before each true sentence.

1. _____ Scribes were well-educated Jews who studied and explained God's law.

2. _____ The commandments are seven signs of God's presence.

3. _____ To value a law is to believe it is important.

4. _____ We can love God without loving other people.

5. _____ To love God is the greatest commandment.

6. _____ Reverence is an attitude of respect, care, and honor.

7. _____ Jesus said we should love ourselves more than anybody else.

8. _____ The Sabbath is a day for rest and prayer.

9. _____ Pharisees did not think God's laws were important.

10. _____ Mercy is loving concern or compassion.

Write one of the Ten Commandments that shows our love for God.

_____

_____

Write two of the Ten Commandments that show our love for others.

1. _____

_____

2. _____

_____

UNIT **4** REVIEW

Complete each sentence by writing the correct word. Then circle the number of each corporal work of mercy and underline the number of each spiritual work of mercy.

1. Forgive _____.

2. Visit those in _____.

3. _____ the sick.

4. Be _____ with others.

5. Shelter the _____.

6. Give _____ to the thirsty.

7. _____ those who are hurting.

8. Pray for the _____ and the dead.

Match the people listed in Column A with their achievements listed in Column B.

Column A

A. Angela Merici

B. Dorothy Day

C. Father Damien

D. Jesus

Column B

_____ worked among lepers on an island called Molokai

_____ started *The Catholic Worker* newspaper and Catholic Worker houses for the poor

_____ taught about the importance of love

_____ taught young girls and brought comfort and hope to their families

COMMUNICATION SKILLS for PROBLEM SOLVERS

To *communicate* with someone means to give him or her information. Being able to give someone information about how you feel and what you need is an important part of problem solving. It is important to be aware that your tone of voice, your body posture, and your words all work together to send information about how you feel. Sometimes your tone of voice gives a message that is different from the message your body posture gives. And it is always important to choose your words carefully. This could help avoid confusion.

Activity Communication Choices

Look at the two illustrations below. Circle the number of the illustration that you think better communicates what the person with the problem is trying to say.

Everyone knows that **IGNORING SOMEONE** can be a helpful solution when that person is teasing you. Look at the following illustrations. Circle the number of the picture that shows the person who is doing the best job of ignoring.

Asking for help is sometimes the best solution to a problem. We cannot always solve our problems all by ourselves. But knowing *when* to ask for help and when to try to solve the problem on our own is sometimes hard to figure out. For example, nobody wants to be called a tattletale, but sometimes telling an adult about a problem is very important or may even be necessary.

Activity When to Ask for Help

Look at the pictures below. Circle the number of the picture that shows a problem that requires asking for help.

1.

2.

Problem Solving Reminders

1. Remember to stop and think.
2. Think of as many solutions as you can.
3. Think about the consequences of a solution before trying the solution.
4. If the first solution does not work, try another.
5. If you cannot get any solutions to work, have trouble thinking of any solutions, or the problem is dangerous for you or others, seek help from an adult.
6. Remember that Jesus is always with you. Pray to Jesus, and ask him for his help.

Following Jesus

In Luke 6:27–36, Jesus tells us that we are to love our enemies. If we love only those who love us, we are not doing all that we can do as Christians. So even when people treat us in ways that make us angry or uncomfortable, we should try to communicate with them in a loving way.

PRAYER

Write a prayer to Jesus and ask for his help with a problem you are having a hard time solving. Use one of the following sentences to help you begin.

Jesus, I wish I could _____.

Jesus, please help me with _____.

Jesus, my biggest problem is _____.

Jesus, I'm sad. Please help me figure out what

to do about _____.

OPENING DOORS
A Take-Home Magazine™

Growing Closer

YOUR FAMILY PROBABLY HAS SOME WONDERFUL STORIES to tell! Keep these stories alive by telling them often to one another. Reminisce about a favorite relative or friend. By telling the story over and over again, your family will remember that special person or event and keep the memory alive from one generation to the next.

WRITE A FAMILY LETTER or telephone a relative or friend who has moved away. Allow everyone to contribute a few lines of news, a local newspaper article of interest, or a drawing. Tell the person receiving the letter or phone call how your family remembers him or her even though you may not often be together.

Looking Ahead

Four major categories of ministry were evident in the earliest Christian communities. They are extensions of Jesus' own ministry. Unit 5 will deal with these four categories: ministries of the word, ministries of building community, ministries of worship or liturgy, and ministries of service.

THIS IS OUR FAITH

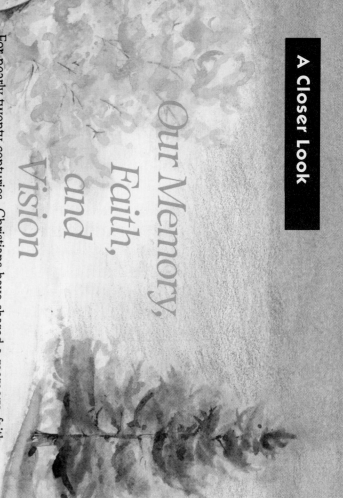

A Closer Look

Our Memory, Faith, and Vision

For nearly twenty centuries, Christians have shared a memory, faith, and vision. We have been called to *celebrate* his presence with us now, and to *remember* what Jesus did for us, to *believe* and trust that we share in the resurrection of Jesus.

In the Memorial Acclamation at Mass, we proclaim the mystery of Jesus' passion, death, and resurrection, and of his coming again in glory. Called not only to remember but also to make present this mystery, the Church unites herself with Jesus in the eucharistic celebration.

In Judaism and Christianity, remembering is more than nostalgic recollection. It is a reenactment of the event recalled. The Jewish people remember in this way when they share the Passover Seder. In this ritual meal, special foods help Jews remember in a vivid manner some of the most important events in Jewish history. They eat unleavened bread as a reminder of their hurried flight from their captors. They eat a claylike mixture of apples, nuts, and wine to remind them of the mortar their ancestors used to build bricks while they were slaves to the Egyptians.

2

After Alice's many persistent visits with officials, Monmouth County had its first shelter for the homeless.

A short time later, when Alice saw abandoned houses being bought by developers and leveled to makes space for luxury condos and other businesses, she sought to secure some of those abandoned houses for the poor. Alice Kelsey is still pursuing her goal to have every community along the Jersey shore donate one abandoned house to be suitably repaired and then purchased at an affordable rate by a low-income family. Working just enough hours to support herself, she reserves plenty of time to devote to the poor.

Poverty and pain respect no age or geographic boundaries. In northeastern Wisconsin, Father "Marty" Carr operates a shelter called *The Place 2B.* Centered in a repossessed motel in Oshkosh, this ministry serves runaway teenagers, mothers and children from abusive families, transients, and many other homeless persons. The hospitality includes not only shelter and food but also counseling services and recreation. An ongoing food pantry, daily meals, and special holiday meals serve hundreds of area residents.

Among the many volunteers at *The Place 2B* are area teenagers who want to do their part. They might cook or serve meals, run errands, or simply listen to the concerns of those teens seeking help or companionship. The recreational facility also meets the needs of these teens to simply come together with their friends. With the support of many churches, the facility for Father Carr's ministry has truly become "The Place To Be!" Like Alice Kelsey, he and his helpers show us that a heritage of caring continues when the followers of Jesus work together to make a difference!

7

When Catholics remember Jesus in the eucharistic liturgy, we do much more than just recall the first time Jesus gave his body and blood to his disciples. We believe that Jesus gives himself to us again each time we share the Eucharist.

"Christ has died, Christ is risen, Christ will come again."

Through the eyes of faith, we recognize Jesus' living presence in the Eucharist and celebrate the life-giving strength we receive. We believe that because Jesus rose from the dead, our lives, too, will be transformed by God.

Like the Eucharist, hope is a gift that we not only receive but also make present "as we wait in joyful hope for the coming of our Savior, Jesus Christ." And like Jesus, we proclaim the promise of the kingdom not only with words but also with our lives. When we gather to *remember* and *celebrate*, and when we love and serve one another, we keep alive the vision of new and eternal life that we *believe* we have already begun to share!

A Heritage of Caring Continues

Belgian Father Damien de Veuster sacrificed his health and life to work among the lepers at Molokai, Hawaii. Saint Francis of Assisi gave to the poor even the clothes he was wearing. Saint Elizabeth of Hungary was forced to give up living as a princess in a castle because she persisted in helping the poor people in the hospitals she had built at the edge of her castle property.

In today's society, it still takes a real commitment to help the poor and forgotten. How can such difficult situations be helped? The opportunities to do so are often very close to home. Two remarkable individuals who have spent the better part of their lives generously meeting the challenge to serve others in this way are Alice Kelsey and Father Martin P. Carr.

Alice Kelsey is an advocate for the homeless who believes in getting things done. After learning that the homeless in affluent Monmouth County, New Jersey, did not have a place of refuge, Alice moved quickly to find help. She discovered that two years earlier a U.S. Army post had offered the county a barracks for the homeless.

A Gift to Remember

Jesus asks us to remember him when we gather together to share the meal he has provided for us. Work through these pages with your child. Help your child appreciate Jesus' request that we remember him by sharing in the Eucharist and by being Christ for one another.

Imagine that your best friend has moved away. You feel sad, lonely, and discouraged. All of those favorite games you played together and all of those special places where you spent time together no longer feel or look the same. "I'll never forget you" and "Write to me" become very important words at this disappointing time.

Jesus and his friends may have felt the same kind of sadness when the time came for him to leave them. Before he died, Jesus gave his friends a very special way to

remember him. He blessed, broke, and shared bread with them. And they shared a cup of wine. After telling them that this food and drink were his body and blood which would be broken and given for them, Jesus told his friends to remember him whenever they shared this food and drink. He also promised to be with them always, even after he died. Whenever Jesus' friends gathered together to remember and to celebrate, Jesus was with them. As Jesus' friends we, too, remember Jesus when we share this special gift, this holy food. We, too, remember that Jesus is with us in a special way in the Eucharist.

Sharing in the Eucharist is one very important way we remember Jesus. But there are many other ways, too. Fill in the activity below with ways you can remember Jesus. The first one is done for you.

I remember Jesus when I *am kind to others.*

I remember Jesus when I _____.

I remember Jesus when I _____.

I remember Jesus when I _____.

I remember Jesus when I _____.

I remember Jesus when I _____.

I remember Jesus when I _____.

When you go to Mass, listen for the words of Jesus that ask us to remember him whenever we gather for Eucharist.

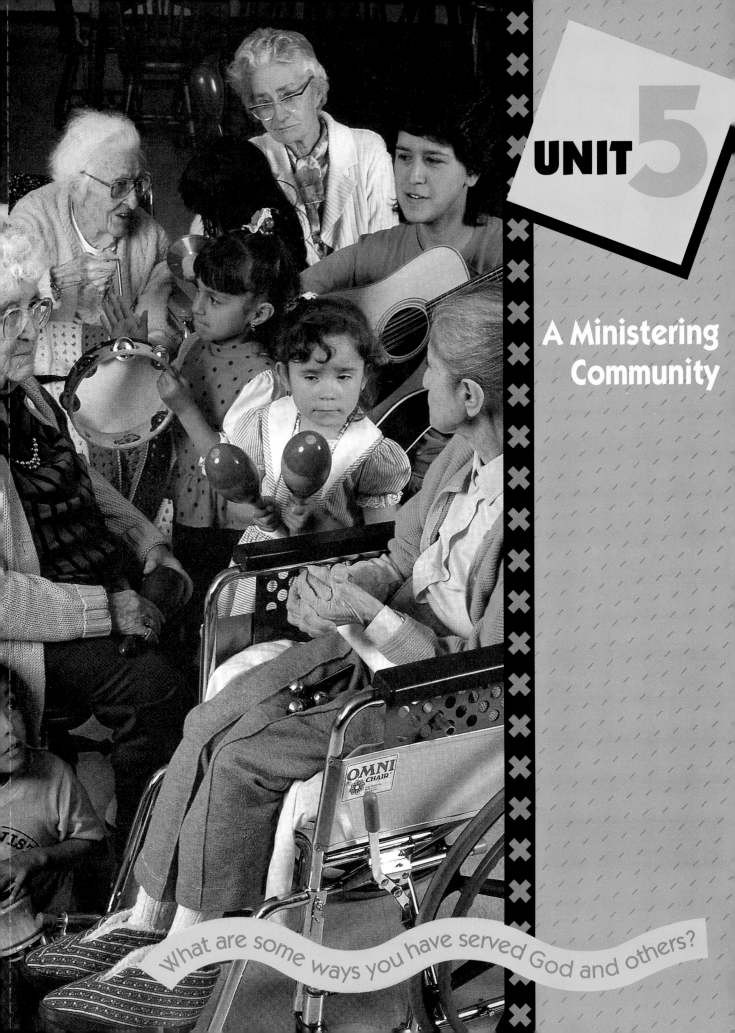

UNIT 5

A Ministering Community

What are some ways you have served God and others?

17

Our Church Builds Community

What are some things that help people live, play, study, and work together in unity?

Pulling Together

The Kowalski family had never gone camping before. All six family members—Mom, Dad, Grandpa, Jane, Tony, and Michael—climbed out of their minivan at the campsite in the hills. Everyone but Grandpa began exploring the area.

They walked into the woods, and they soon discovered a stream. Within a few minutes, they saw a deer, three squirrels, and six kinds of birds. Tony and Jane tripped over fallen branches. After half an hour in the woods, Mom, Dad, Jane, Tony, and Michael were hungry. They went back to their campsite.

Grandpa had snacks set out for them. While they ate, they planned how they would set up the tent, prepare dinner, and tell stories around the campfire after dark.

"Dad and I can set up the tent if Grandpa will start organizing everything for dinner," Mom suggested. "Then we can all cook the food together."

"The boys and I can get wood for a fire," Jane volunteered.

All agreed and set to work. Everything went almost as planned. Dad and Mom got the tent up, but it took longer than they thought. Grandpa set the table and prepared the corn, hot dogs, and hamburgers for cooking. Jane, Tony, and Michael found plenty of logs and branches for the fire, but only a few dry ones.

Together they cooked the food and enjoyed their dinner. The campfire sputtered and smoked more than it burned, but the stories were wonderful, as each person took a turn speaking.

Soon it was time for the Kowalskis to start thinking about getting settled into their sleeping bags in the tent. As Jane poured water on the fire, she said, "We haven't had this much fun together as a family for a long time." They all agreed!

Jesus Builds Community

Jesus had worked hard to bring people together. So much of his **ministry** was aimed at building community, especially among people who had faith in God.

Today the Church continues Jesus' **ministry of community building**. Communities grow when people use their gifts and talents for the good of the communities to which they belong. We are each called to use our gifts to help the Church community and other groups, such as our families, to grow in unity. We also welcome and encourage the gifts that other people bring to the Church and to these groups.

Vocabulary

ministry: the ways we serve God and all people according to God's special call

ministry of community building: ways in which we help the Church to grow in unity

✘ ✘ ✘ ✘ ✘ ✘ ✘ ✘ ✘ ✘ ✘ ✘ ✘

One Body, Many Members

Paul was one of the leaders of the early Church. He was called to be an apostle after Jesus' death and resurrection. He helped begin the first Christian communities in many cities. And like Jesus, Paul worked hard to bring people of faith together as God's children.

Later, Paul and his partners wrote letters to those churches. Many of the letters became part of the Bible. Here is what one letter says about the Church and our part in it.

"There are many ways to serve God. There are many things to do. The Holy Spirit gives each person special gifts and talents to use for the good of all.

"We have all been baptized into one body. The Church is like a single body made up of many members. We need them all—hands, feet, eyes, and ears. The parts are many and different, but the body is one. The eye cannot say to the hand, 'I don't need you.' The head can't say to the feet, 'I have no need of you.'

"God made the body so that all its parts have concern for one another. If one part is hurt, the whole body shares the pain. If one part is honored, the whole body shares the joy.

"Now you are part of Christ's body, the Church. Each one of you has a part to play in the whole."

Based on 1 Corinthians 12

The Church Builds Community

Jesus worked to build community wherever he went. Today the Church continues Jesus' ministry of community building. In the sacrament of Baptism, we are all made members of Christ's body, the Church. As we grow in faith, we come to understand that all members of the Church are called to share in the ministry of community building.

Some people are called through the sacrament of Holy Orders to be leaders in this important ministry. A **pastor** is a priest who leads a parish community. He is often assisted by other priests and professional lay ministers as well as lay volunteers in the task of building unity in the parish. A parish may also have a **deacon**, who is ordained to help the priest in serving the parish community in many different ways.

A parish community is part of a **diocese**, which is a larger community of many parishes that are located near one another. As pastoral leader of a diocese, a **bishop** works to build community among many parishes and between his diocese and the worldwide community of Catholics. The **pope**, bishop of Rome and leader of the Catholic Church all over the world, helps the worldwide Catholic community to grow in peace and harmony. The Catholic Church builds community not only among its own members but also with other Christian churches throughout the world.

Vocabulary

pastor: a priest who leads a parish community

deacon: a person ordained to help the priest in serving the parish community in many different ways

diocese: a community of many parishes that are located near one another

bishop: pastoral leader of a diocese

pope: bishop of Rome and leader of the Catholic Church all over the world

✖ ✖ ✖ ✖ ✖ ✖ ✖ ✖ ✖ ✖ ✖ ✖

Activity

Each member of the Church is called to help people live in harmony with one another.

Our pastor is _____ .

Our bishop is _____ .

Our pope is _____ .

We Believe

Jesus is with us to unite us as a community of his followers. He calls us all through Baptism to share in his ministry of building community.

Activity

Consider the groups or teams you belong to and the things that you enjoy doing. Think about the qualities you have that can help you show teamwork and support for these groups or teams.

Use the letters that spell your first name as the first letters of words that describe some qualities you have. Follow the examples for *Sam* and *Pat*.

Strong   **P**eaceful

Athletic   **A**rtistic

Musical   **T**alented

_____

_____

_____

_____

_____

Ministries in Scripture ~~~

In Paul's letters to the early Christian churches, he often gave instructions to the Church leaders. He wrote about the qualities that Church leaders should have. They were to be people whom others could respect; they were to be sincere, gentle, peaceful, and responsible. They were to be people who could bring people together as a community of believers and help them to be united. To learn more of what Paul wrote about Church leadership, read 1 Timothy 3:1–13.

In one part of his letter to the Philippians (Philippians 1:3–11), Paul gave thanks to God for all the people who shared in the ministries of the Church and who supported Paul, Timothy, and other Church leaders. He told them that they were all partners in sharing the gospel with others. And he prayed that their faith and their love would increase.

Activity

Complete the paragraph below to describe some of the gifts of people in your parish who share in the ministry of community building. Then write a prayer for these community builders and share this prayer aloud. Know that your prayer is also part of this ministry.

One Church leader whom I admire as a good community

builder is _____ because

_____ .

I believe that one way I can help bring together the

people at _____ parish is to

_____ .

I can also help build community in my own family by

_____ .

My Prayer for the Community Builders in My Parish and My Family

_____

_____

_____

_____

_____

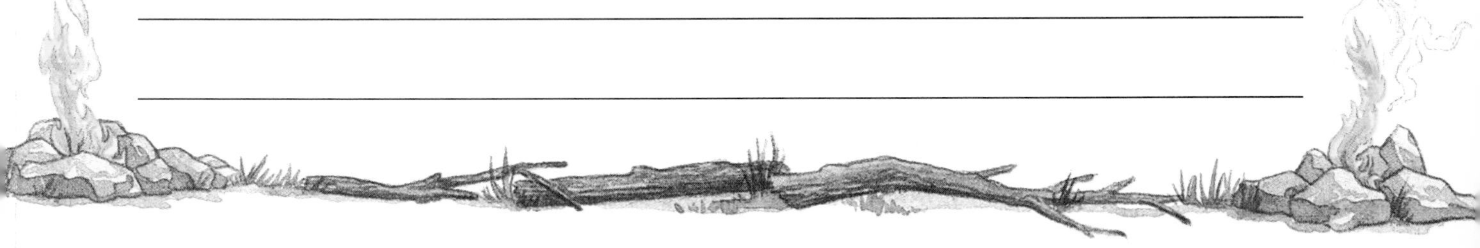

One Flock, One Shepherd ～～～

One day, Jesus was talking to a large group of people. They were confused and upset. They wanted to follow Jesus, but some people had said bad things about him.

Jesus wanted to build this community. So he told them a story about himself and about themselves.

"Sheep gather around their shepherds," Jesus said. "When the shepherd calls the sheep by name, they follow him. They know who he is because they recognize his voice."

Everyone knew how sheep flocked together around their shepherds. There were shepherds all over their country.

"I am the good shepherd," Jesus told them. "I know my sheep and they know me. I protect them from the dangers that scatter them. I keep my sheep together as a flock."

Jesus paused for a moment. Then he continued. "There are other sheep who are not yet part of my flock. I will call them and lead them together. Then there will be one flock and one shepherd."

Based on John 10:1–18

Discuss

1. How would you respond to someone who made fun of your beliefs, your Church, or your family?

2. What are some of the things that we say or do that could cause us to become separated from our brothers and sisters in Christ?

3. What things could we say or do to bring people back together once they have been separated from one another?

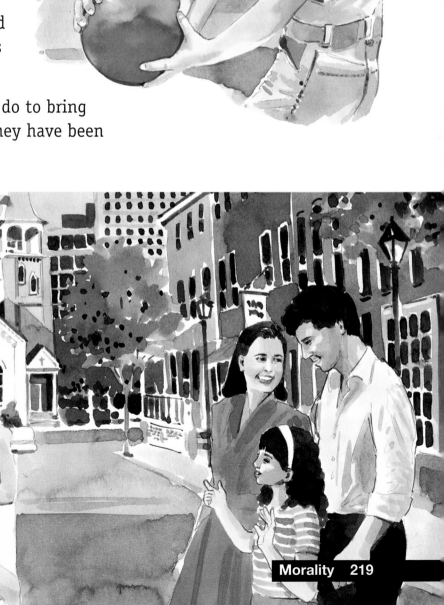

Praying for Our Communities

Leader: As we pray today, we remember that we belong to many communities—the communities of our families, our school, our parish, our diocese, our cities and towns, our nation, and the world. We pray today especially for the community builders in our own families, our school, and our parish. Let us pray.

Leader: Holy Spirit, you call us to serve the members of our own families.

All: Help us to respect our parents as they bring our families together to share all the good things that families can share.

Leader: Holy Spirit, you call us to serve one another in our school and in our parish community.

All: Help us to support our parish leaders, our pastor, our principal, and our teachers in their ministry of building community.

Leader: Holy Spirit, you call us to make every effort to be united. May our prayers today be a sign of all the efforts that we will continue to make to help build unity in all the communities in which we live. Guide us in our prayer each day so that we might remember to pray for one another always.

All: Lord God, help us to serve you and all your people by using the gifts you have given us. Help us to use these gifts to build up the community of Christ's body, the Church. Amen.

Chapter Review

For each word in Column A, write the letter for its definition from Column B.

Column A

_____ **1.** bishop

_____ **2.** ministry

_____ **3.** pastor

_____ **4.** diocese

_____ **5.** pope

_____ **6.** deacon

_____ **7.** ministry of
community building

Column B

a. leader of the whole Catholic Church

b. pastoral leader of a diocese

c. ways we serve God and all people

d. community made up of many parishes

e. helping the church to grow in unity

f. priest who leads a parish community

g. a person ordained to assist in
serving a parish community

Fill in the answers to the first two questions.

1. What is the *ministry of community building?*

_____

_____

2. What special role does the pope have in the

Church? _____

_____

3. Talk about where, how, and with whom you
can help build community.

**Do everything
you can to
be united in
the Spirit.**
Based on
Ephesians 4:3

18

Our Church Preaches God's Word

Share a story about a time when something you said helped someone feel better.

Dear Patty,

Thank you for writing back so soon. All the kids in the neighborhood miss you very much. You are so much fun! We wish you could be here with us for the <u>whole</u> summer!

Are you having a good time? What kinds of things are you doing? Does your dad have a piano for you to play? You did such a great job at your recital last month!

Sorry to hear you got the chicken pox from your little brother. We hope you feel better soon! Please write back soon. We can't wait to see you at school this Fall.

Your friend,
Katie

P.S. Nicole has two new kittens. I hope you like the picture her Mom took of all of us. Do you have any pictures you could send us?

Discuss

1. What words in Katie's letter might Patty have especially appreciated?

2. How do you think Patty will respond?

3. What words would mean the most to you if you got a letter like this?

Jesus Brings Us God's Word

Jesus often used words to help people. He began his ministry using God's word. He said he was going to bring God's message to all people. He was planning to teach and preach. He was sent to be a minister of God's word.

Christ continues to bring us God's word through the Church's **ministry of the word**. As members of the Church, we all share in this ministry. But we can only share what we ourselves have received.

Activity

Circle the two verses that you would most like to share with someone.

"*I will be with you always.*"

Based on Matthew 28:20

"*Do not be worried or afraid. I give you my peace.*"

Based on John 14:27

"*I will never forget you.*"

Based on Isaiah 49:15

"*You can do anything with God's help.*"

Based on Mark 10:27

With whom would you share these messages?

We Believe

The Church today continues Jesus' ministry of the word. Each of us is called to share God's word with others and to live its message.

Jesus Speaks God's Word ⁓⌒

Jesus grew up in a Jewish family, who often prayed together and talked about the Scriptures they heard at the synagogue and Temple. Jesus' hometown was Nazareth. He sometimes read the Scriptures in the synagogue there.

One Sabbath day, Jesus was in the synagogue at Nazareth. He unrolled the scroll of the **prophet** Isaiah until he came to a special passage. He read the following words out loud.

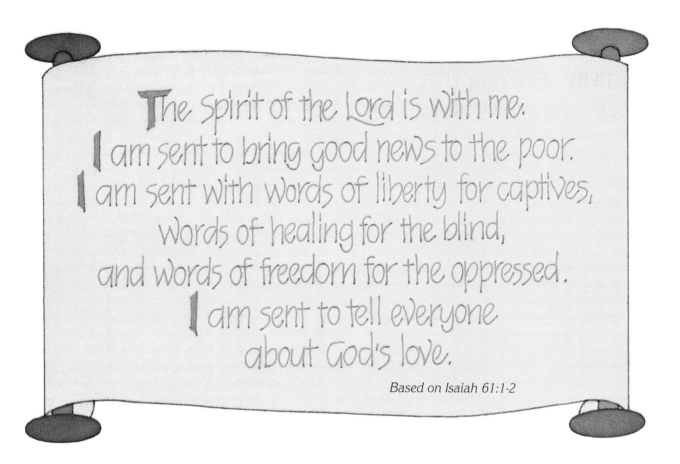

The Spirit of the Lord is with me.
I am sent to bring good news to the poor.
I am sent with words of liberty for captives,
words of healing for the blind,
and words of freedom for the oppressed.
I am sent to tell everyone
about God's love.

Based on Isaiah 61:1-2

Then Jesus said, "Today, these words of the Scriptures have come true in me." The people in the synagogue were amazed at Jesus' words. They could not believe that this man was the boy who had grown up right there in Nazareth.

Based on Luke 4:16–22

Jesus *Is* God's Word

Jesus said that he was sent by the Father to bring God's word to all people. Jesus' ministry of teaching and preaching helped the people understand how much God loved them. They came to know Jesus as a great storyteller, teacher, and prophet. They also came to know Jesus as God. Jesus said to them, "Now that you know me, you also know and see the Father" (based on John 14:7).

Vocabulary

prophet: someone called by God to speak in his name

✖ ✖ ✖ ✖ ✖ ✖ ✖ ✖ ✖ ✖ ✖ ✖

Activity

Read each sentence. Write words that a friend or another person might say to help someone in each situation. Use your own words or select words from the word wall below.

1. "I keep trying, but I can't do these math problems."

_____

2. "I'm sorry I called you names."

_____

3. "It seems as if nobody likes me."

_____

4. "I'm afraid I'll make a mistake if I try."

_____

"I forgive you."

"Forget about it."

"I know how to do that. I'll teach you."

"I feel the same way."

"I like you just the way you are."

"You're cool!"

"I know what you mean."

"You can do it! I know you can."

God's Word in My Parish

Each of the following pictures shows a familiar way that God's word is shared in a parish. A **lector** is a minister of the word who proclaims God's word at Mass. A religion teacher helps us understand God's word. A priest or deacon invites us to live God's word when he preaches the homily at Mass.

Vocabulary

lector: a minister of the word who proclaims God's word at Mass

✖ ✖ ✖ ✖ ✖ ✖ ✖ ✖ ✖ ✖ ✖ ✖

Paul, a Minister of God's Word

Paul was a minister of God's word who served the early Christian communities. He helped to begin some of these communities. He often returned to visit these communities, and he visited many others as well. He shared the gospel everywhere he visited by preaching God's word to the people.

Whenever he was not traveling, Paul wrote letters to the Christian communities. We call his letters that became part of the New Testament in the Bible the **epistles**. Paul's epistles were often filled with words of joy and hope. Even when Paul was in prison, he wrote letters to encourage the early Christians to keep on living as Jesus wanted them to.

Paul's letters were filled with words that helped people remember what Jesus had taught. He reminded them that Jesus wanted them to live in unity and to be patient with one another. He reminded them that Jesus wanted them to live according to God's laws and that loving God and others were the most important commandments. In reminding the early Christians what Jesus had taught, Paul often helped them settle arguments about how they were called to live as people of faith.

I HOPE TO VISIT YOU SOON SO WE CAN ENCOURAGE EACH OTHER IN THE FAITH.

When ministers of the word read from or teach about God's word today, they also remind Christians of who they are called to be. They also remind us that God loves us and is always with us. They encourage us to be strong in our faith and to keep on learning and growing as faithful Christians.

Activity

Each of us can share in the ministry of the word in helpful ways. Think of one person who would like to hear words of love or peace, hope or comfort, encouragement or forgiveness. Select one of the sentences from the Scriptures. Add your own words to these words of God. On the pad, write a message to the person you think needs to hear it.

"I will forgive you."
Based on Jeremiah 31:34

"I will never forget you."
Isaiah 49:15

"Do not be afraid."
Matthew 14:27

"I am with you always."
Matthew 28:20

"My love shall never leave you."
Isaiah 54:10

"Take courage and be strong."
Daniel 10:19

Vocabulary

epistles: the letters, written mostly by Paul, that became part of the New Testament in the Bible

✖ ✖ ✖ ✖ ✖ ✖ ✖ ✖ ✖ ✖ ✖ ✖ ✖

Praying with the Lectionary

Leader: The Church has given us a great gift to help us understand God's word more clearly. Today, as we listen to a reading from the *Lectionary for Masses with Children*, let us pray that we will all do our part in sharing God's word.

Reader: A reading from the holy gospel according to Mark.
Some people brought their children to Jesus so that he could bless them by placing his hands on them. But his disciples told the people to stop bothering him.
But when Jesus saw this, he became angry and said, "Let the children come to me! Don't try to stop them. People who are like these little children belong to the kingdom of God. I promise you that you cannot get into God's kingdom, unless you accept it the way a child does."
Then Jesus took the children in his arms and blessed them by placing his hands on them. (From the *Lectionary for Masses with Children*, Weekday Reading No. 207)
The gospel of the Lord.

All: Praise to you, Lord Jesus Christ.

Leader: Let us pray. Lord God, we thank you for Jesus and for Church leaders who want all of us to hear and understand your word and your love for us. Give us the courage and the opportunity to share in the Church's ministry of the word so that we can spread the word about your love for us and for everyone.

All: Amen.

Chapter Review

Use the clues below to fill in the crossword puzzle.

Down

1. Someone called by God to speak in his name
2. Helps the priest in serving the parish community
4. A minister of the word who proclaims God's word at Mass

Across

1. A minister of God's word who served the early Christian communities

3. Each of us is called to _____ God's word with others and to live its message.
5. Someone who invites us to live God's word when he preaches at Mass
6. Serving others by sharing God's word with them is sharing in the _____ the word.

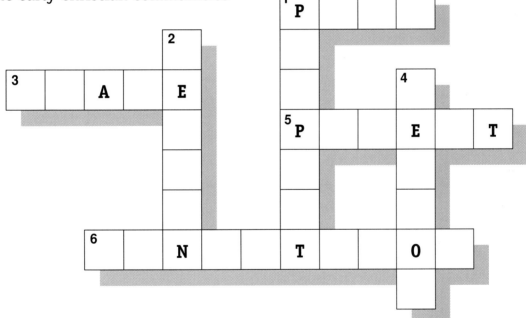

Fill in the answers to the first two questions.

1. What is the *ministry of the word*? _____

   _____

2. Who continues Jesus' ministry of the word

   today? _____

3. Talk about more ways you can bring God's word to people.

> **Share God's word, in good times and bad times.**
> **Based on**
> **2 Timothy 4:2**

19

What are some things you like about praying with others at home? In class? In church?

Our Church Worships God

Praising God

Jesus prayed many kinds of prayers. We have already learned about the psalms Jesus prayed from the Scriptures. When Jesus wanted to say how wonderful his Father is and how grateful he was, Jesus said a prayer of **praise**. When we say a prayer of thanks, we usually thank God for something or someone very specific. We might say, "Thank you, God, for beautiful flowers!" When we say a prayer of praise, we may just want to say, "God, you are so wonderful!" And then we may want to tell God all the reasons we believe this!

Activity

On the lines below, make a list of some events, people, places, or things for which you would like to praise God. Put a check next to one that is especially important to you right now.

_____

_____

_____

Discuss

1. What are some ways to praise God?

2. Have you ever praised God when you were by yourself? When?

3. What are some times and places you have praised God together with others?

Praising God in Song

Long before the time of Jesus, Jewish people entered their Temple singing a short psalm or hymn. In Psalm 100, the people of Israel call upon all the nations of the world to join with them in praising God. Psalm 100 also praises God who created us and who remains faithful to us forever.

A Processional Psalm

Everyone, come and sing to the Lord!
Serve the Lord happily!
Praise the Lord with happy songs!

May we never forget that we belong to God.
We can say to the Lord,
"We are your people, we are your flock!"
We enter the temple gates with thanksgiving
    and praise.

Bless the name of the Lord, who is so good to us!
Our Lord's kindness and faithfulness last forever!

Based on Psalm 100

Vocabulary

praise: a way to show or tell God how wonderful we believe he is and how grateful we are to him

✖ ✖ ✖ ✖ ✖ ✖ ✖ ✖ ✖ ✖ ✖ ✖

Praying Together

Jesus prayed regularly with his friends in their homes, in synagogues, and in the Temple in Jerusalem. After his death and resurrection, Jesus' friends and followers continued to pray together. They gathered regularly in the Temple to **worship**, or to give honor and praise to God. They often prayed together in their homes, too.

Paul, an important leader among the first Christians, wrote letters to Jesus' followers in many cities. He often encouraged them to praise and thank God in worship together. These are his words to two early Christian communities.

Dear faithful ones in Ephesus,

Sing psalms and hymns and spiritual songs among yourselves, singing and playing music to the Lord in your hearts. Give thanks always and for everything in the name of our Lord Jesus Christ to God the Father...

Based on Ephesians 5:20

Dear friends in Philippi,

Don't worry about anything, but ask God for what you need and want. Pray to God with thankful hearts. Then God's peace will be with you...

Based on Philippians 4:4–9

The Ministry of Worship

The Church today continues to worship God. We gather together to give praise and thanks, to ask for God's help, to ask for forgiveness of our sins, and to pray for others. We pray together in devotions and in the liturgy, the Church's official community prayer. Every baptized Catholic is called to take an active part in the Church's worship, especially the Eucharist. We can help others to pray, too. There are many ways we can serve our parish communities through the **ministry of worship**.

Our Worship Experience

We are called to give honor and praise to God, both alone and with others. Catholics all over the world gather in communities to worship God. The pictures below show some familiar ways we can share in the ministry of worship.

Activity

Write the names of people who serve in these ministries at your school or parish Masses.

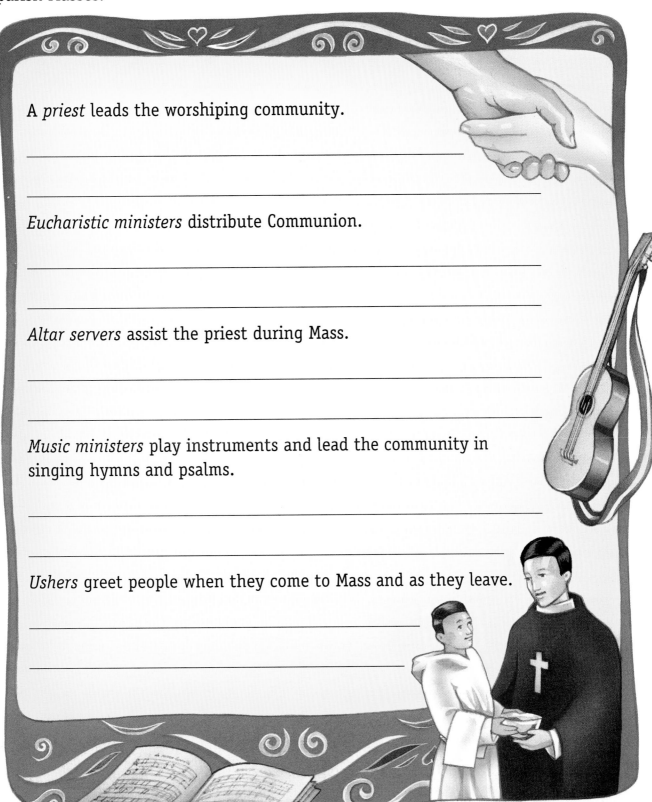

A *priest* leads the worshiping community.

_____

_____

Eucharistic ministers distribute Communion.

_____

_____

Altar servers assist the priest during Mass.

_____

_____

Music ministers play instruments and lead the community in singing hymns and psalms.

_____

_____

Ushers greet people when they come to Mass and as they leave.

_____

_____

Jesus Gives Praise to the Father

One day, Jesus went off by himself to think and to pray. For months he had been telling people about God's love. For months he had been reaching out to people who were sick or poor or troubled.

But it seemed that only a few people really listened to Jesus. Not many people seemed to be changing their lives and opening their hearts to God and others in response to Jesus.

Some educated and powerful people were turning away from him. The leaders of the Temple were actually against him. Jesus wondered if all his work was for nothing.

The only people who seemed to change their lives because of Jesus were some of the poorest and least educated people. These simple people seemed to sense that God was actively working through Jesus.

As Jesus thought about this, he felt sad and discouraged. He wished that more people would listen to him and understand his words and actions. Then his thoughts turned to God.

Jesus knew that God was with him. He believed God was part of what was happening. So he prayed, "Father, Lord of heaven and earth, I praise you. I thank you for showing to the simple people what the educated and powerful refuse to understand. Father, in your goodness, you have a reason for it to be this way" (based on Matthew 11:25–26).

An Attitude of Praise

Jesus teaches us that we can always have an attitude of praise because God is always wonderful to us and blesses us. When we show that our hearts are always ready to praise God, we can encourage our friends and our families to have faith, even when they may feel sad or discouraged. This kind of encouragement can help people to pray during times when they may not feel like praying.

Praying for a Blessing on the Ministers

Leader: Our prayer today is a prayer of praise to God for the ministers of worship in our school. Let us begin our prayer with Psalm 149:1–2.

Group 1: Sing to the Lord a new song of praise!

Group 2: Come, all you faithful children of God!

All: God, you are so wonderful to us! We praise you now and always!

Group 1: Be happy because God is good!

Group 2: Come, rejoice in your king and Lord!

All: God, you are so wonderful to us!
We praise you now and always! Amen!

Based on Psalm 149:1–2

Reader: A reading from Paul's letter to the Ephesians. (Student reads Ephesians 5:20 from page 235 of the student text.)

Leader: As your name is read, please come forward to receive a special blessing on your ministry of worship.

Teacher: (to each minister of worship) I praise God for you, _____.
May God bless you and guide you to always serve the Lord with gladness! (Please respond: Amen.)

Leader: Let us pray.
Lord, we thank you for the gifts and talents that all of these special people use to serve you in this school community. As they help us to pray, fill them with hearts of praise to lead us in celebrating your unending love for us.

Ministers: We thank you for calling us each by name. We thank you for the gifts you have given us. Help us to use them to encourage others in their faith. And keep our faith strong always. Through Jesus Christ our Lord.

All: Amen.

Chapter Review

Unscramble the word(s) to complete each statement. The words appear in order.

1. To _____ God is to show or tell him how wonderful we believe he is.

2. _____ encouraged the first Christians to worship God together.

3. To give honor and praise to God, especially as a community, is to _____.

4. To help people to pray and take part in community worship is a _____ of worship.

5. Two ways we can share in the ministry of worship are as a _____ minister and as an _____ server.

| ispare |

| uaPl |

| psworih |

| ystiminr |

| smiuc |

| atarl |

Fill in the answers to the first two questions.

1. What does *worship* mean? _____

_____

2. What are some forms of the ministry of worship? _____

_____

_____

3. Talk about your own experiences of worship.

Come, let us worship the Lord who made us.
Based on Psalm 95:6

20

Our Church Serves

People in Need

There are people in need all around us. Sometimes friends, neighbors, or members of our own families are hurting. Sometimes those in need may be strangers.

There are sick people without medicine or doctors. There are women and men who want to work but cannot get jobs. There are people who are treated badly because of how they look or what they believe. There are people who have no family, too little to eat, or nowhere to live. Some people have needs so great that it takes the work and love of many people to help meet those needs.

Activity

Listed in this puzzle are five ways that people suffer. The words read across and down. Circle each word. On the lines next to the puzzle, write about some other ways that people suffer in the world today.

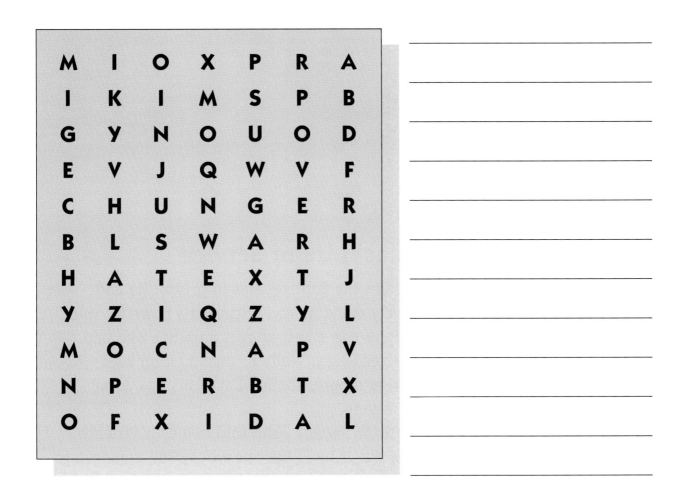

M	I	O	X	P	R	A
I	K	I	M	S	P	B
G	Y	N	O	U	O	D
E	V	J	Q	W	V	F
C	H	U	N	G	E	R
B	L	S	W	A	R	H
H	A	T	E	X	T	J
Y	Z	I	Q	Z	Y	L
M	O	C	N	A	P	V
N	P	E	R	B	T	X
O	F	X	I	D	A	L

_____

_____

_____

_____

_____

_____

_____

_____

_____

Jesus' Message of Service

Throughout history, there have been people in need. Jesus knew that much suffering was caused by selfishness and greed. So he not only helped people who were suffering but also spoke out against those who caused the suffering. Jesus brought a message of love, **justice**, and peace to victims of injustice. He taught us to treat everyone fairly and with respect.

Vocabulary

justice: treating everyone fairly and with respect

✗ ✗ ✗ ✗ ✗ ✗ ✗ ✗ ✗ ✗ ✗

Jesus' Life of Service

John the Baptizer was in prison. He had bravely stood up and criticized a powerful ruler.

John was a well-known preacher who had baptized Jesus. While in prison, John kept hearing reports about what Jesus was doing and saying.

"Go to Jesus," John told two of his friends. "Ask him if he is the one whom God promised to send to help us in our need."

So the two went to look for Jesus. They found him surrounded by a crowd of people.

"John the Baptizer sent us to ask you a question," they told Jesus. "Are you the one God promised to send to help us? Or should we look for someone else?"

Jesus answered by pointing to some of the many needy people he had helped. Some had been blind, deaf, or lame. Most were poor. Jesus said, "Just look around you. Go back and tell John what you have seen and heard."

Then Jesus recalled words from the Scriptures to show that he was the one whom God had promised to send: "The blind are able to see. Crippled people can walk straight again. Deaf people can now hear. People who were dead have new life. And the poor have received the good news of God's love." Then Jesus said, "Happy are those who place their faith in me."

Based on Luke 7:18–23

The Church's Ministry

Jesus spent his life serving others. He reached out especially to those who were poor, weak, sick, hungry, and homeless.

The Church today continues Jesus' works of love, justice, and peace among all God's people. All Catholics are called to the **ministry of service**—reaching out to people in need and working to change situations and attitudes that cause pain and suffering.

Vocabulary

ministry of service: reaching out to people in need and working to change situations and attitudes that cause people's pain and suffering

✖ ✖ ✖ ✖ ✖ ✖ ✖ ✖ ✖ ✖ ✖ ✖

We Believe

Jesus spent his life serving people in need. He calls us to share in his ministry of love, justice, and peace.

Discuss

1. What stories have you read about people in the world who are in need?

2. How do these stories make you feel?

3. How could you use your gifts to help carry someone else's burden?

A Friend of the Poor

One cold, snowy evening a young soldier named Martin was riding his horse through a town in France. He pulled his warm cloak around himself as the wind whistled and whirled.

At the city gate, Martin saw a man begging. The man had no warm clothes. He looked as if he were freezing.

Martin drew his sword, took off his warm cloak, and cut his cloak in half. He gave half the cloak to the beggar and wrapped the other half around himself.

That night, Martin dreamed that he saw Jesus Christ wearing the half of his cloak that he had given to the beggar. Soon after, Martin decided to spend the rest of his life serving and caring for people who were poor.

Years later, Martin became the bishop of Tours. Each year on November 11, the Church honors Saint Martin of Tours as a friend of the poor and a model for those who help people in need.

Our Ministry of Service

We are called through Baptism to share in Jesus' ministry of love, justice, and peace. When we use the special gifts and talents we have been given to serve our brothers and sisters who are in need, we are answering God's call.

Many people help or serve people who are poor or in need. People help others for many different reasons. When we help others because we are following God's call, what we do is a ministry of service. When we share in this ministry, we recognize the many needs that people have. People who are homeless, for example, need more than shelter. They also need the love and care of people who will listen to their stories, who will not judge them, and who will treat them with respect.

Activity

Look through some newspapers or magazines. Cut out a picture that shows someone in need.

Write about one way you can reach out to this person. Show the picture to your group as you share what you wrote.

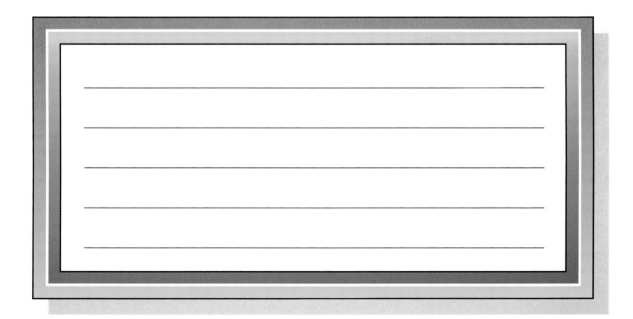

Activity

Look at the list of people below. Next to each category, write someone's name and describe one way you can reach out to and care for that person.

Family member: _____

Neighbor: _____

Friend: _____

Classmate: _____

Covenant House

Covenant House is one of many organizations in the United States today that share in the Church's ministry of service. Located in many large cities throughout the United States, Covenant House helps America's homeless teenagers. Covenant House workers first help these teenagers by giving them food, clothing, shelter, and medical care. Covenant House workers also minister to the teenagers by teaching them to trust in the love and care that the community offers.

Covenant House workers talk to the runaway teenagers to help them deal with all kinds of problems. The ministers of service at Covenant House show by their actions that God loves each and every person in need. They help the teenagers to find jobs or to finish school. Covenant House workers recognize that people who are suffering often have needs that affect their minds, hearts, and spirits as well as their bodies.

Activity

Look through a newspaper or magazine. Find a story or picture about people serving others. Paste it in the space below. On the lines provided, write about the many ways that these people are being helped.

ⲛⲛ 𝕹𝖊𝖎𝖌𝖍𝖇𝖔𝖗𝖍𝖔𝖔𝖉 𝕹𝖊𝖜𝖘 ⲛⲛ

Vol. 21-No. 12   Daily Edition

PEOPLE SERVING OTHERS

Praying for the Church's Ministry of Service

Leader: As Catholics who share in Jesus' ministry of service, let us pray for the courage and the wisdom to do all we can to work for justice as we help people who are in need.

Leader: Lord, give your Church wisdom to see and courage to meet the needs of our own families, especially _____.

All: Lord, we are the Church! We are the ones you call to this service.

Leader: Lord, guide your Church in its efforts to meet the needs of people and situations in our community, especially

_____.

All: Lord, we are the Church! We are the ones you call to this service.

Leader: Lord, lead your Church to bring the good news of your love to all the corners of the earth, using the many gifts, talents, and resources with which you have blessed us.

Help others, especially _____, to hear and be encouraged by the prayers of your faithful servants.

All: Lord, we are the Church! We are the ones you call to this service.

Leader: Lord, guide us in all our efforts to serve others with loving compassion and respect. And Lord, when we are the ones who are suffering or in need, give us the grace to accept the love of those who minister to us. Amen.

Chapter Review

Complete the sentences by writing word(s) from the border.

justice   injustice   needs   war   hate

1. Five ways people suffer are _____

_____ .

2. _____ is treating others fairly and with respect.

3. Reaching out to people in need and working to change situations that cause

people's suffering are ways of sharing in the ministry of _____ .

4. _____ was a friend of the poor.

5. Covenant House workers meet many different _____ of
America's homeless teenagers.

hunger   poverty   service   Saint Martin of Tours

Fill in the answers to the first two questions.

1. What is *justice?*_____

_____

2. Who were some of the people in need whom

Jesus helped?_____

_____

3. Talk about what you can do to help someone in
need or to work for justice and peace.

**Put your gifts at
the service of
one another.**
Based on 1 Peter 4:10

UNIT 5 ORGANIZER

In each box below, identify some people who share in this ministry and describe what each person does.

Ministry: ways we serve God and all people according to God's call

Community Building

_____

_____

_____

_____

_____

Word

_____

_____

_____

_____

Worship

_____

_____

_____

_____

Service

_____

_____

_____

_____

_____

UNIT **5** REVIEW

Match the words in Column A to the definitions in Column B.

Column A

1. ministry
2. pope
3. prophet
4. praise

Column B

_____ someone called by God to speak in his name

_____ thanking God for being wonderful

_____ the ways we serve God and all people according to God's special call

_____ the leader of the Catholic Church all over the world

Circle the letter of each correct answer.

1. Today, the _____ continues Jesus' ministry of the word.

   (a) scribes   (b) Church   (c) government

2. The Holy Spirit helps us work to live in _____ and harmony.

   (a) wealth   (b) anger   (c) unity

3. Jesus taught his friends and followers to _____ God.

   (a) find   (b) forget   (c) worship

4. Jesus spent his whole life _____ people in need.

   (a) serving   (b) needing   (c) ignoring

5. Jesus calls us to share his ministry of love, justice, and _____.

   (a) power   (b) peace   (c) preaching

Name the four ministries of the Church.

_____   _____

_____   _____

Find the hidden words in the puzzle that Jesus spoke about. The first letter of each word is given. Write the words on the answer lines.

```
L  I  F  V  L  I  N  E
F  O  R  G  I  V  E  A
N  H  E  A  L  I  N  G
P  E  R  H  O  P  E  X
E  X  D  O  R  A  L  R
A  L  O  V  E  H  A  S
C  O  M  F  O  R  T  T
E  M  S  T  R  A  N  G
```

F __ __ __ __ __ __   L __ __ __

H __ __ __ __ __ __   H __ __ __

C __ __ __ __ __ __   P __ __ __ __

Name four ways to serve in the ministry of worship.

_____   _____

_____   _____

FEELING LEFT OUT

Fitting in and belonging to a group is not always easy. Some of us may feel that we have no close friends. Some of us may feel that the friends we were once close to no longer care about us. The person who is our best friend today may be best friends with someone else tomorrow. We are beginning to learn that friendships sometimes change.

When we experience changes in friendships, we have many different feelings and often react in a variety of ways. If we feel angry and resentful, we may want to get back at those who have hurt us. Some of us may be good at pretending everything is fine, yet on the inside we feel sad and lonely.

Some of us may try to keep our hurt from showing by being silly or acting tough. Sometimes when we feel left out, we can easily forget that we were created by a loving God who never forgets us or leaves us.

Karen's Problem

Karen is a new student in the third grade. She is having a hard time making friends and is feeling very lonely. Part of the reason things are so difficult for her is that she is shy and unsure about how to make friends. The other kids are not unkind. They just do not seem to notice her. She is never picked to be someone's partner and is usually alone at recess. Some of the kids spend time on the weekend at each other's houses, but Karen is never invited. Karen wishes she could go back to her old school. When her mother asks her how things are going, she pretends to like her new school so that her mother will not worry.

Activity Finding a Solution

Use your problem-solving skills to complete the chart below and find the best solution for Karen.

Karen's problem: _____

Karen's goal: _____

Possible solutions	Possible consequences
_____	_____
_____	_____
_____	_____

REMINDERS WHEN FEELING LEFT OUT

1. Share your feelings with someone who will listen.

2. Use your problem-solving skills to think of some good solutions.

3. Participate in activities that give you a chance to meet new friends and also keep you busy with something fun to do.

4. Reach out to others and let them know that you are interested in being their friend.

5. Be a good friend. Remember to listen. Be willing to share and take turns.

6. Remember that Jesus cares about you and loves you, especially when you are feeling unloved by others.

Following Jesus

Jesus always looked out for people who were feeling left out. We know that he looks out for us, too, when we feel this way. Jesus wants us all to care for one another in the same ways that he cares so that nobody feels left out.

PRAYER

Jesus, help us to choose the best words and actions that show our care for others, especially for those who are lonely. Amen.

OPENING DOORS
A Take-Home Magazine™

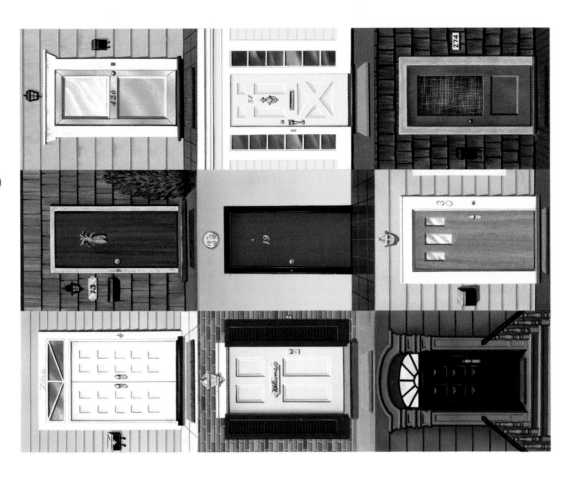

THIS IS OUR FAITH

Growing Closer

TRY TO FIND a few minutes each week to read the Scriptures, either alone or with your family. Rediscover how the word of God challenges you to bring the message of Jesus to others.

MAKE IT A FAMILY PRACTICE to discuss Sunday's gospel together. Allow the gospel message to speak personally to you. Encourage one another to live out the challenge of Jesus' words and example.

Answers for pp. 4–5: Mass, Church, or Eucharist • sabbath • Sunday • God or Jesus • Scriptures or Eucharist • pray • sing • praise • God or Jesus

listen • Scriptures • lector • Old Testament • New Testament • psalm • priest or deacon • priest or deacon • gospel

homily • message

ministry • love, healing, guidance, forgiveness, peace, strength, comfort

• Church • people

Looking Ahead

As the summer approaches, take time to recognize God in your midst. Each time your family is gathered together and each time you join the family of Jesus to celebrate together, remember that "where two or three are gathered together in my name, there am I in the midst of them" (Matthew 18:20).

The Book of Psalms

"The precepts of the Lord give joy to the heart."

adapted from Psalm 19:9

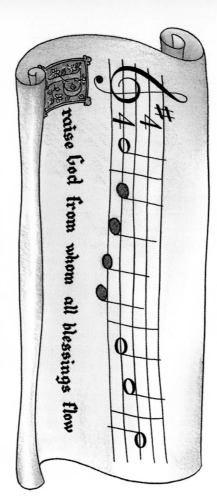

raise God from whom all blessings flow

Helping us to take the word of God to heart, the psalms, a book of 150 songs from the Old Testament, have become an important part of the Liturgy of the Word. Sung or recited after the First Reading, the psalm is related to the other readings proclaimed at Mass. The psalm, however, serves a more meditative purpose. It gives the worshiping community an opportunity to think about and respond to God's word by helping to maintain a prayerful pace, or flow, in the liturgy.

Because of the range of sentiments found in them, the psalms are often the point where our life stories connect with the story of God's salvation. For the Hebrew psalm writers, the events of their lives were very much a part of this story of the whole people of God. Even though written from a personal perspective, they have long been prayers of the whole community.

Paul himself became a hunted and persecuted man—someone seen as a traitor by some Jewish leaders.

Called to preach the good news wherever it had not yet been proclaimed, Paul was constantly on the move. He would stop in a town or city for a short while, preach the gospel, baptize converts, and leave behind trained disciples to lead the new community as he traveled on. Because Paul cared deeply about each of the churches he founded, he was dedicated to writing letters of encouragement to them. In addition, whenever Paul heard of one of the new Christian communities experiencing a problem, he would attempt to correct the situation by reminding the people of who they were called to be as followers of Jesus.

Paul's first epistle was addressed to the Thessalonians, urging them to continue growing in patience, faith, and love until Jesus came again in glory.

At Galatia, there was a major argument about whether or not Gentile converts had to become Jews before they could become Christians. Paul tried to settle the issue in his letter to this community by emphasizing that salvation was by faith in Jesus and not determined by circumcision or any other law.

The illicit lifestyle of many Christians in Corinth and the lack of unity among members of the worshiping community were among the concerns of the Corinthians which came to Paul's attention. Thus, in his letter to the Corinthians, Paul dealt with proper Christian conduct and described the Church as the body of Christ whose members needed to work together.

When we read the letters of Paul today, it is important to keep in mind the historical reasons why they were written. As in all Scripture, however, the truths revealed in Paul's letters are as timeless as the God who inspired them!

While about one third of the Psalms are lamentations, or cries of distress, many more are festive hymns of praise or thanksgiving to the God of salvation. The Hebrew word for psalms is *tehillim*, which means "praises." Written over a period of 1,000 years, the psalms tell the praises of the people of God and of their faith in God's presence and power in all aspects of life.

"Come before the Lord with joyful song!"
adapted from Psalm 100:2

The Psalter, or Book of Psalms, was probably the hymn book used in Jewish worship as early as the sixth century B.C. So we should not be surprised to see many references to the psalms in the New Testament. Jesus sometimes alluded to the psalms when he was teaching or praying. In the reading of the passion at the Palm Sunday liturgy, we hear Jesus reciting from a psalm about trusting God (Psalm 22:2): "My God, my God, why have you abandoned me?" In the parable of the tenants recorded in Mark 12:1–12, we find Jesus comparing the "beloved son" (verse 6, probably indicating himself) to "the stone which the builders rejected" which became "the cornerstone" (Psalm 118:22). Psalm 118 is the Responsorial Psalm used in the Easter Sunday liturgy.

So a tradition of nearly 3,000 years of worship continues. In fact, it is believed that most of the psalms were written specifically for the purpose of prayer and worship. The Hebrew *tehillim* have been used effectively in both Jewish and Christian liturgy for many centuries!

Being Catholic

The Letters of Paul

Do you still take the time to write letters to long-time friends? If so, then you know that letters often can have more impact than a phone call. Letters can be read again and again. They can be saved and savored.

One of the most famous of all letter writers in the Scriptures is Saint Paul. Before his conversion, Paul was a religious bigot. He persecuted Christians as traitors to Judaism. After his conversion,

... LET US NOT GROW TIRED OF DOING GOOD, FOR IN DUE TIME WE SHALL REAP OUR HARVEST ... LET US DO GOOD TO ALL

Sharing the Message

The Liturgy of the Word is an important part of the Mass. God speaks to us through the Scriptures, telling us of God's love and of our responsibility to each other as children of the same Father. As you work through these pages with your child, rediscover both the gift and the challenge the word of God is to us as Christians.

We go to ———— on the Christian ———— day, which is ————. ———— shares himself with us in the ————. We ————, we ———— songs, and we ———— God for all the wonderful things ———— has done for us.

We also ———— to the ————. A person called a ———— usually reads a story from the ———— part of the Bible and a story from one of the letters found in the ————. In between these two readings, we say or sing a ————.

Now it is time to stand and welcome Jesus among us as the ———— or ———— reads a ———— story to us. Sometimes the gospel story is difficult to understand. The priest or deacon gives a special talk called a ————.

This helps us better understand the ———— of the gospel story. Just as Jesus' ———— was to bring God's word to everyone he met, we too share in the ministry of the word. God's word brings people ————, ————, ————, and ————. Through us, the ————, God's word is brought to all of God's ————.

Some of these words can be used more than once.

Church	praise	Jesus	Eucharist
forgiveness	sabbath	Mass	guidance
healing	pray	Old Testament	lector
listen	sing	New Testament	message
ministry	Sunday	priest	peace
people	deacon	Scriptures	
psalm	gospel		
strength			
comfort			
God			
homily			
love			

Listen carefully to the Scripture readings the next time you go to Mass. Try to share the message of God's word with others this week.

Celebrating the Journey

Leader: We are the Church! We believe that by worshiping together, we keep faith alive in our hearts. We believe that by serving together, we keep Jesus Christ alive in the world.

Reader: A reading from Paul's letter to the Ephesians.

Leader: Our journey together has led us to this peaceful moment where we can rest, pause to remember, and be refreshed and strengthened for the journey ahead. Let us bless one another now with this water, which reminds us of the life of Jesus born in each of us at Baptism.

Leader: Our faith has been renewed as we have seen Jesus in one another and in all the people of

———————————————————————

parish. Let us profess our faith together now as we join hands and recite the Apostles' Creed.

Leader: Let us pray.

All: God, we thank you for the Holy Spirit who came to give life to us, your Church. We thank you for each other and for another year of growing and learning together. Keep us close to you and to one another. We ask this in Jesus' name. Amen.

Our Church Celebrates Advent

The Jesse Tree

When Jesus was a little boy, he learned about people who lived long ago. He loved to hear his mother, Mary, tell the stories of his ancestors.

He learned about Abraham, the first great leader of God's people. He listened to the story of Moses leading God's people through the desert. He heard the story of Noah, who saved his family from a great flood. And he enjoyed singing the psalms of King David.

During the season of Advent, we remember some of the people on Jesus' family tree. Each of them helped to make things ready for Jesus to come into the world at Christmas time. Jesus' family tree is called the **Jesse Tree**.

To help us remember the ancestors of Jesus, we draw a symbol for each person and hang it on a tree branch. Noah's symbol might be a boat, and David's symbol might be a musical instrument.

Activity

Choose four members of *your* family. In the boxes below, draw a different symbol for each person. Then write the name of the person beneath his or her symbol.

Jesus' Ancestors

The Bible told people that a great leader would come from the family of Jesse. Jesse lived a long time before Jesus. He was the father of King David. Both Jesse and King David were Jesus' ancestors.

Jesus had many ancestors. Some of them are listed below. Read the list and look at the symbols. Then look at the Jesse Tree banners on page 264. Find the symbols for these ancestors and talk about them with your class.

	Abraham: God said his children and grandchildren would be as many as the stars.
	Jacob: He dreamed about angels going up and down a ladder to heaven.
	Moses: He was a great leader of God's people. God gave him stone tablets on which the Ten Commandments were listed.
	Mary: She was the mother of Jesus.
	Joseph: He was a carpenter. He loved and cared for Mary and Jesus.

Activity

Fill in the blanks to complete the missing words. Then use these words to fill in the puzzle below. When you have completed the puzzle, you will find the name of a special Advent activity.

1. ___ ___ ___ ___ __s__ is our Savior.

2. Moses was a ___ ___ ___ __d__ ___ ___ of God's people.

3. ___ ___ ___ ___ ___ __h__ was a carpenter.

4. We celebrate Jesus' birth on

   ___ ___ __r__ ___ ___ ___ ___ ___ ___.

5. We __p__ __r__ ___ ___ ___ ___ ___ for Christmas

   during ___ ___ ___ ___ __n__ ___.

6. There are ___ __o__ ___ ___ weeks in the Advent season.

7. Noah and King David were

   ___ ___ __c__ ___ ___ ___ ___ ___ ___ of Jesus.

8. ___ __e__ ___ ___ ___ was the father of King David.

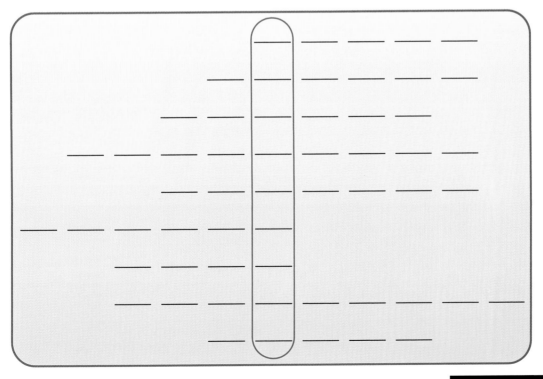

John the Baptizer

John the Baptizer was an important part of Jesus' family tree. John's parents, Elizabeth and Zechariah, were kind and loving people who wanted to have a child. But for many years, they were sad because they did not have a child.

One day, God sent an angel to Zechariah. The angel said, "Elizabeth is going to have a son. Name him John. He will prepare the way for God's Son, Jesus."

Elizabeth and Zechariah were filled with joy when John was born. They taught John to love God and to follow God's ways.

When John grew up, he went to the desert to pray and study. Then God called him to be a **prophet**, a messenger who speaks for God. God told John to tell people to prepare for Jesus' coming.

John traveled from town to town. He baptized many people and told them, "Change the way you are living. Be baptized. Prepare the way for the Lord."

John told everyone how to get ready for Jesus. He said, "Share your food and clothes with the poor. Be sorry for your sins. Tell the truth. Be happy with what you have. Believe in the good news!"   *Based on Luke 1:5–17; 3:1–14*

Activity

During Advent, we prepare the way for Jesus by doing kind things for others. We try to treat everyone with love and care. Learn the signs that tell us what God wants us to do during Advent.

Prepare

the way

for

the Lord.

Making a Jesse Tree

There are many different kinds of Jesse Trees. On page 264, there are two photographs of Jesse Tree banners. The symbols were cut from cloth and then pasted to large cloth banners.

You can make another kind of Jesse Tree by following the directions below.

A Tree-Branch Jesse Tree

1. Find a large tree branch that has already fallen from a tree.

2. Stand the branch in a large can filled with sand, dirt, gravel, or pebbles.

3. Use construction paper to make the symbols.

4. Each week during Advent, add a few symbols for Jesus' ancestors.

5. Use yarn or thread to hang the symbols on the branch.

6. As you place the symbols on the tree, remember how Jesus' ancestors helped prepare the way for Jesus to come into the world. As you hang the symbols on the tree each week, you may want to use the prayer service on the next page.

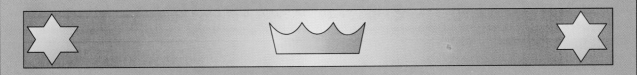

Advent Prayer Service

Teacher: As our ancestors did long ago, let us prepare the way of the Lord. Listen carefully to these readings from the Bible.

Reader 1: The Lord says, "The time is coming when I will keep my promise to send a great ruler. He will do what is right and just. When he comes, everyone will be safe."

Based on Jeremiah 33:14–16

Reader 2: When the great king comes, he will be from Jesse's family. He will be wise and strong. He will know and do God's will. He will stand up for the poor and bring peace and justice to all the nations.

Based on Isaiah 11

Reader 3: Shout for joy, O children of God! Sing a glad song in your hearts. Your king is already among you. God will make you new in his love.

Based on Zephaniah 3:14–17

Reader 4: The Lord says, "City of Bethlehem, listen! Everyone thinks you are too small. But the ruler of Israel will be born within you. He will be like a good shepherd. He will bring peace to the whole world."

Based on Micah 5:1–3

All: Loving Father, we remember that your Son, Jesus, was born on Christmas. We need Jesus in our world today. Help us to get ready for him to come to us again. Amen.

Our Church Celebrates Christmas

A Christmas Play

Reader 1: Long ago, the Emperor sent out a letter ordering everyone in the whole world to be counted. So Joseph, who was a descendant of King David, went to Bethlehem, the hometown of David. Joseph's wife, Mary, went with him.

Reader 2: While they were in Bethlehem, the time came for Mary to have her baby. Joseph looked for a place for Mary to rest. He went to talk to the innkeeper.

Joseph: My wife is going to have her baby. Can we stay in your inn?

Innkeeper: There is no room here. My inn is filled with travelers who came to be counted. You and your wife may stay in the stable.

Reader 3: So Joseph and Mary stayed the night in the stable. And on that night, Mary's son was born. She wrapped him in soft clothes and put him in an animal's feeding tray to sleep.

Reader 4: Out in the fields, shepherds were guarding their sheep. Suddenly, the sky was filled with bright light, and an angel of the Lord appeared to the shepherds. They were frightened. The angel said:

Angel: Don't be afraid! I have good news! Your Savior has been born today. You will know who he is because you will find him in the stable in Bethlehem.

Reader 5: Suddenly many other angels from heaven appeared and began praising God. They said:

Angels: Glory to God in heaven! And peace to God's people on earth!

Reader 6: The shepherds hurried to Bethlehem and found Mary and Joseph in the stable with Jesus. Then they returned to the fields, praising and thanking God for all they had seen and heard.

Based on Luke 2:1–20

Activity

Like the shepherds, we can thank God for sending Jesus to be with us. Use the lines below to write a Christmas message of praise and thanks to God.

Adoration of the Magi (oil), Johann Overbeck

The Wise Men

Shortly after Jesus was born, some travelers arrived in the city of Jerusalem. They were wise men who studied the stars. They had followed a bright star. They knew it would lead them to the newborn king of God's people.

The wise men had special gifts for Jesus. They had brought gold and rare spices fit for a king.

In Jerusalem the wise men talked to King Herod. They asked him where Jesus was. Herod asked the chief priests and other leaders about the new king.

"According to the prophets, he was to be born in Bethlehem," they said.

Herod sent the wise men to Bethlehem. They followed the star again until they came to the place where Mary and Joseph and the baby Jesus were. The visitors were so pleased to find Jesus. They bowed down before him. Then they gave him their special gifts. Giving Jesus these gifts made the wise men very happy.

Based on Matthew 2:1–12

Activity

During the season of Christmas, we enjoy giving gifts. The gifts are a sign of our love. When we choose a gift, we try to find something the person needs or will enjoy. We look for a gift that will be just right.

Draw a line to match each gift with an appropriate person. Be sure each person gets a gift.

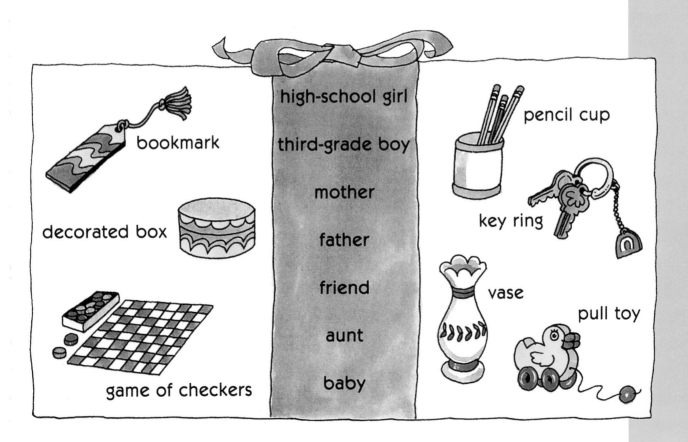

bookmark

decorated box

game of checkers

high-school girl

third-grade boy

mother

father

friend

aunt

baby

pencil cup

key ring

vase

pull toy

The Gifts of the Wise Men

In the Bible we read that the wise men brought gifts for Jesus. One gift was gold. This was a sign that the wise men considered Jesus a king. They were honoring Jesus, their king, with a precious and valuable gift.

Another gift the wise men brought was incense. This gift showed that Jesus is God's Son. We use incense when we pray to and worship God. When the smoke of the burning incense rises up, it reminds us of our love and prayers rising up to God.

The third gift the wise men brought was unusual. In Jesus' time, when a person died, the body would be washed and covered with special perfumes and ointments. One such fragrance was called **myrrh**. The gift of myrrh was a sign that Jesus was human and that someday he would die.

Remembering the Wise Men's Visit

On the Feast of Epiphany, we celebrate the wise men's visit to Jesus and his family. In some countries, people celebrate this day by blessing their homes or asking a priest to do so.

Activity

One of the prayers of blessing is written below. Say the prayer together. Then write your own prayer of blessing for your home. Share your prayer with your family.

May Christ bless our home and stay with us throughout the new year.

A Gift for Your Family

1. On a separate sheet of paper, copy the family prayer below.

   Loving God,
   Help us to live like the Holy Family, united in respect and love. Bring us to the joy and peace of your eternal home. We ask this through Jesus, our brother. Amen.

2. Find a Christmas card with a picture of the Holy Family, or draw your own picture.

3. On a sheet of construction paper, paste your copy of the family prayer and the Holy Family picture.

4. Punch a hole at the top of the construction paper. Then use yarn to hang your gift on your Christmas tree.

5. Say the prayer with your family during the Christmas season.

Loving God,
Help us to live like the
Holy Family, united in respect
and love. Bring us to the joy
and peace of your eternal home.
We ask this through Jesus,
our brother, Amen.

Prayer Service for the Christmas Season

All: We three kings of Orient are,
Bearing gifts we travel afar.
Field and fountain, moor and mountain,
Following yonder star.
O star of wonder, star of night,
Star with royal beauty bright,
Westward leading, still proceeding,
Guide us to the perfect Light.

Reader 1: The wise men brought gold because,
Jesus, you are a king.

All: Jesus, be our king always.

Reader 2: The wise men brought incense because,
Jesus, you are God's Son.

All: Jesus, bring our prayers to God the Father.

Reader 3: The wise men brought myrrh because,
Jesus, you are one of us.

All: Jesus, be our brother forever.

Reader 4: The wise men followed the star,
and they found Christ,
who is the Light of the World.
May we, too, find Jesus in our lives.

All: Amen.

Our Church Celebrates Lent

Jesus Falls a Third Time (oil), Guilio Vespaziani

Stations of the Cross

Many people want to remember the good things that Jesus
did. They want to remember that Jesus died on the cross for
them. Every year during the season of Lent, Christians from
many parts of the world gather at a place near Jerusalem called
Calvary, where Jesus was crucified. They gather to remember the
way Jesus carried the heavy cross up the hill. They remember
how he died.

People who cannot travel to Calvary want to remember Jesus,
too. So they go to church and stand before pictures of Jesus
carrying the cross. They say a prayer at each picture and
remember how much Jesus loves them. The crosses that mark
the stops in this procession are called the **Stations of the Cross**.

Activity

During Lent we can remember Jesus in many ways. List three ways you can remember Jesus.

1. _____

   _____

2. _____

   _____

3. _____

   _____

Now travel with Jesus up to Calvary by writing on each line one thing you will do for others during Lent.

A Time of Reconciliation

After praying and fasting in the desert for forty days, Jesus began his **mission**. A mission is the work God calls us to do. Jesus'

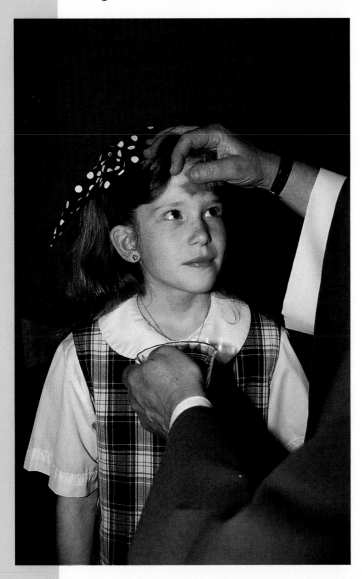

mission was to tell people the good news about God's love for them. When Jesus announced his mission, he said, "Turn away from sin and believe in the good news" (based on Mark 1:15).

On **Ash Wednesday**, the first day of the season of Lent, we receive ashes on our foreheads. As the priest uses ashes to trace the Sign of the Cross on our foreheads, he may repeat Jesus' words from Mark 1:15. Or the priest may say, "Remember, you are dust, and to dust you shall return" (based on Genesis 3:19). The ashes remind us that Lent is a time to change our lives. It is a time to tell God that we are sorry for our **sins**. A sin is choosing to do something we know is wrong. When we sin, we turn away from God's love.

During Lent, God wants us to think about our words and actions. We can think about how we have shown our love for God, Jesus, and others. We can ask ourselves if we have tried to follow God's commandments every day. When we think about all these things, we call this an examination of conscience. Many parishes have special opportunities throughout the season of Lent to think about the ways we may have sinned.

If we have sinned, we can celebrate God's forgiveness in the sacrament of Reconciliation. God will forgive us if we are sorry for our sins.

Lent is a special time to celebrate Reconciliation. In Reconciliation we promise to follow Jesus more closely. As we turn away from our sins and try to grow closer to Jesus, we get ready to share in Jesus' new life, which we celebrate at Easter.

Activity

Think about your words and actions. Then write a prayer to Jesus. In your prayer, tell Jesus one thing you want to change about how you are living and what you will do to try to grow as a follower of Jesus.

Take Up Your Cross and Follow Me

During Lent, we remember that Jesus told his friends what they must do if they wanted to be his disciples. Jesus said, "If you want to come with me, you must forget about yourself, take up your cross, and follow me" (based on Matthew 16:24).

Lent is a time to remember Jesus' sacrifice on the cross. Jesus died and rose to save us from sin and to share his new life with us. When Jesus tells us to take up our cross, he is telling us that we must be willing to make sacrifices for others.

Jesus wants us to think about the needs of other people. He asks us to look for ways to show care for others in special ways during Lent. It is not always easy to make sacrifices, but Jesus promises that he will always help us to follow his example.

During Lent, there are three ways we can follow Jesus. We can pray, fast, and do good works. When we pray, we can ask Jesus to help us be less selfish. We can fast by giving up a favorite snack to remember the people in our world who are hungry. The good works we do are a sign that Jesus is alive in the world today. People can see this through our words and actions.

Activity

Here are some ways you can take up your cross during Lent. Choose three things you will do to show that you are a follower of Jesus.

Share my toys with my brother or sister.

Give up candy or ice cream.

Pray the Stations of the Cross.

Make friends with someone new at school.

Give money to the missions.

Forgive someone who has hurt me.

Do my chores without being asked.

Write a letter to my grandparents.

Treat everyone with love and kindness.

Collect food for the hungry.

Watch less television.

Celebrate Reconciliation.

_____

_____

_____

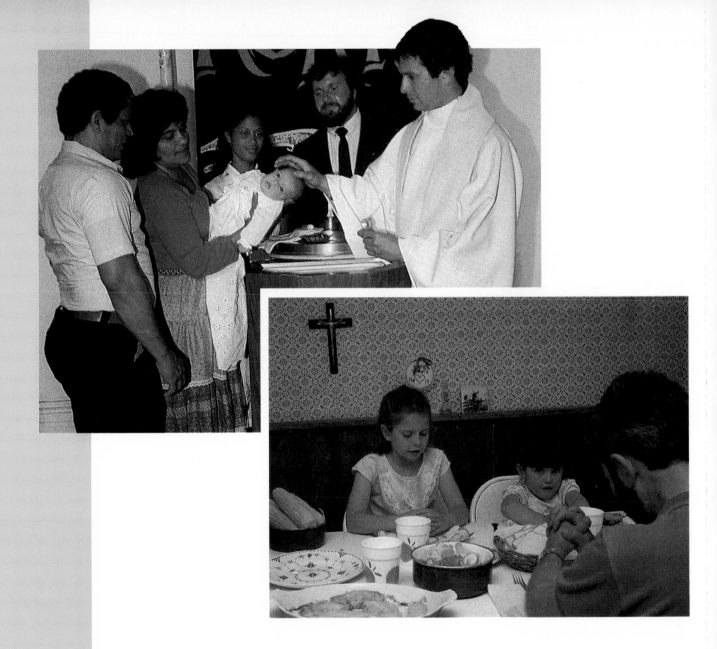

The Symbol of the Cross

Lent is a special season for the Church. During this season, we remember that Jesus suffered and died on the cross. The cross is a Lenten symbol that reminds us of Jesus' great love for us. When we make the Sign of the Cross or when we see a cross, we think of Jesus.

Lent is also a time to remember our Baptism. At Baptism, we are signed with the cross of Jesus. As we remember our Baptism, we should try to be more like Jesus. Lent is a time to grow and to change our selfish ways.

Signs of Victory

The early Christians believed that the cross was a sign of Jesus' victory over death. To them, the cross was a reminder of Jesus' great love.

Many times the early Christians used precious stones, or jewels, to decorate their crosses. Such a cross was called a ***crux gemmata***, or jeweled cross.

Activity

Follow the code to color the *crux gemmata*. Write a motto beside the cross to help you remember Jesus' great love for you.

1 gold	2 orange	3 red	4 blue	5 green	6 purple

Making Crosses

Make one of the three crosses described below and place it in your room at home. Look at your cross often and remember Jesus' great love for you.

1. Find two twigs or sticks. Place one across the other. Wrap purple yarn around the sticks where they cross to hold them together.

2. Cut out a cross from heavy construction paper or cardboard. Glue toothpicks in rows to decorate your cross.

3. Draw a cross on white paper. Use brightly colored crayons to color it. Press hard. Then use a black crayon to cover the entire colored cross. Use a key or pencil tip to scrape off the black to make different designs. The bright colors will shine like a *crux gemmata*.

Prayer Service for Lent

During Lent, Catholics throughout the world pray the Stations of the Cross. They say a special prayer for each station.

After you have finished making the Stations of the Cross booklet on pages 349–352, pray the Stations of the Cross with your class. You may do this in church or in your classroom. Take turns reading the title of each station and talking about what is happening in each picture. Then say together the prayer for each station.

Our Church Celebrates Holy Week

The Triduum

The **Triduum**, the three holiest days of the Church year, is from Holy Thursday evening through Easter Sunday evening. The word *Triduum* means "three days."

On Holy Thursday we remember the Last Supper, when Jesus gave us the Eucharist. During this meal, Jesus took bread into his hands, gave thanks to God, broke the bread, and said, "This is my body, which is given for you. Do this in memory of me." Then Jesus took a cup of wine and said, "This is my blood. Do this in memory of me" (based on 1 Corinthians 11:23–25).

During Mass on Holy Thursday, the priest and other ministers may wash the feet of people in the parish community. In this **ritual**, we remember that Jesus washed the feet of his apostles. And we remember that Jesus calls us to serve others as he did. In a ritual, we use words, actions, and gestures to remember or celebrate something very meaningful.

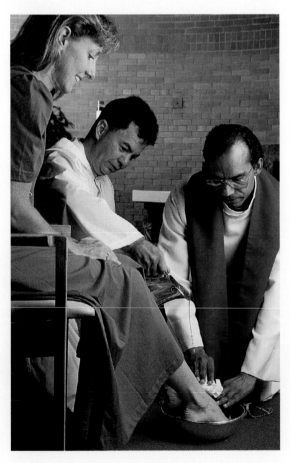

On Good Friday, we remember the day Jesus died. There are no Masses on Good Friday. Instead, we go to church to hear the story of Jesus' death on the cross.

Later, we show our love for Jesus by kissing a special cross. We can also kneel before the cross or touch it gently. Then we all receive the Eucharist.

On Holy Saturday, we remember Jesus' promise to rise from the dead. At night, we go to church for the celebration of the Easter Vigil, when we welcome new members into the Church. Everyone holds a lighted candle. This is a sign that Jesus has risen and that Jesus' new life shines throughout the world.

Activity

Fill in the missing letters in the sentences below.

1. The __T__ ____ ____ ____ ____ ____ ____

   includes the three holiest

   __d__ ____ ____ ____ of the Church year.

2. On __H__ ____ ____ ____ Thursday

   we remember the

   __L__ ____ ____ ____'s Supper.

3. On Good __F__ ____ ____ ____ ____ ____ we remember that

   Jesus died on the __c__ ____ ____ ____ ____.

4. On Holy Saturday, at the __E__ ____ ____ ____ ____ ____

   Vigil, we celebrate new __l__ ____ ____ ____

   with __J__ ____ ____ ____ ____.

The Crucifixion (oil), Hendrick Krock, 18th century

Good Friday

During **Holy Week**, the week before Easter, we remember the important events of the last week of Jesus' life on earth.

The day that Jesus was crucified on the cross is called Good Friday. That is the day that Jesus carried his cross up the hill to the place known as Calvary. Ever since that time, the cross has been a special symbol to all Christians. It reminds us of Jesus, the Son of God, who died on Good Friday and rose to new life at Easter.

We celebrate Christ's Passion on Good Friday. We hear a reading from the Gospels that we call the Passion of our Lord Jesus Christ. *Passion* means "suffering."

On Good Friday we pray this prayer.

Lord,
Send your blessing on us,
  for we remember that Jesus died on the cross
  and rose to new life on Easter Sunday.
Forgive us and help us.
Make us strong in our faith
  so that one day we, too, will share
  that risen life with Jesus and with you,
  forever and ever.
Amen.   Based on the Prayer over the People
                              from the Good Friday Liturgy

Activity

What do you know about Holy Week, the week
that begins with Palm Sunday and ends with
Easter? Write your answer to each question below.

1. What happens on Palm Sunday? _____

_____

2. Why is Holy Thursday important? _____

_____

_____

3. What are some ways we can remember the events of Good Friday?

_____

Our Church Celebrates Easter

Jesus Is Risen

Early on the first day of the week, Mary Magdalene and another woman went to visit Jesus' **tomb**, where his body had been placed when he died. Suddenly an earthquake shook the ground, and an angel of the Lord appeared. The angel rolled back the stone from the front of the tomb and sat on it. The men guarding the tomb were so afraid that they began to shake.

The angel said to the women: "Do not be afraid! I know that you are looking for Jesus who was crucified. He is not here. He has risen, just as he promised. Come and see the place where they put his body. Then go quickly to tell his disciples that he has been raised."

The women hurried away from the tomb to tell the disciples the good news. They were filled with joy and fear. Suddenly Jesus stood before them and greeted them. The women fell down in front of him, touched his feet, and worshiped him. Jesus said, "Do not be afraid. Go and tell my disciples to go to Galilee, where they will see me."

Based on Matthew 28:1–10

On Easter we celebrate Jesus' resurrection. The empty tomb is a sign that God's love is even more powerful than death. God promises that those who love and follow Jesus will share his new life forever.

Activity

Just as Jesus asked Mary to tell the other disciples the good news of his resurrection, Jesus calls us to be his messengers of good news today. Write a heading announcing Jesus' resurrection. Then write how you feel about Jesus' rising to new life.

The Good News Times

ᗰᗰᗰ ᗰᗰ ᗰᗰᗰᗰ   ᗰᗰ ᗰᗰ ᗰᗰᗰ ᗰᗰᗰᗰ ᗰᗰᗰᗰ

_____   _____

_____   _____

_____   _____

_____   _____

_____   _____

Congratulations

ᗰᗰ ᗰᗰᗰᗰ ᗰᗰ ᗰᗰᗰᗰᗰ   ᗰᗰᗰᗰ ᗰᗰ ᗰᗰᗰ ᗰᗰᗰ
ᗰᗰᗰᗰ ᗰᗰᗰᗰ ᗰᗰᗰ   ᗰᗰ ᗰᗰᗰᗰ ᗰᗰᗰᗰᗰ
ᗰᗰᗰ ᗰᗰ ᗰᗰᗰᗰ   ᗰᗰᗰᗰ ᗰᗰ ᗰᗰᗰ
ᗰᗰ ᗰᗰᗰᗰᗰᗰ ᗰᗰᗰ

The Road to Emmaus

After Jesus died, his family and friends were sad. They thought Jesus was gone forever. Jesus had promised to be with them again, but that seemed too good to be true.

On Sunday, two of his friends were walking on the road to a town called Emmaus. As they walked along, another man began to walk with them. They did not know who he was.

"What are you talking about?" the man asked the two friends.

They stopped walking. One of the friends of Jesus said, "Are you the only person who does not know what has happened these past few days?"

The man who had joined them began to talk about Jesus. He helped them understand why Jesus had died.

When they arrived at Emmaus, the friends of Jesus invited the man to stay for supper. After they sat down, the man took a loaf of bread, blessed it, broke it, and gave them each a piece. Suddenly they knew who the man was.

Based on Luke 24:13–35

Activity

Who was the man who joined the apostles on the road to Emmaus? Find and color the hidden words to discover the answer. Hint: Look for two words.

Signs of Jesus' Love

While walking to Emmaus, Jesus' friends did not
know that the man they met was Jesus. But when the
man broke bread and shared it with them, they
recognized Jesus.

We are friends of Jesus. We want to recognize Jesus in
our lives, too. The risen Jesus comes to us in many ways.

When we pray, Jesus is close to us. When we celebrate
the Eucharist at Mass, Jesus comes to us in a special way.
When we read the Bible or study our religion, the words
of Jesus and his teachings become part of us. At home, at
school, and with our friends, the love and care of parents,
teachers, and other good people are signs of Jesus' love
for us.

Discuss

1. During the past week, who were the people who helped you?

2. Who were the people who were kind to you?

3. Who were signs that Jesus was with you?

Activity

Unscramble the letters on each butterfly to find a way that we can bring Jesus' love to others. Write each word on the line provided.

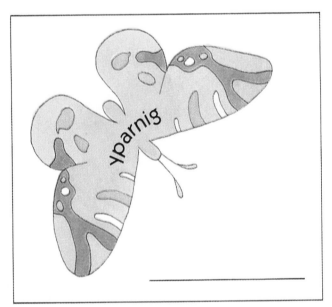

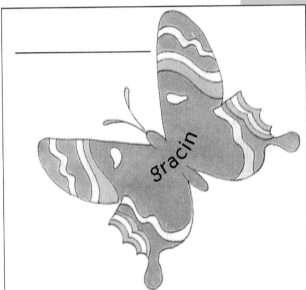

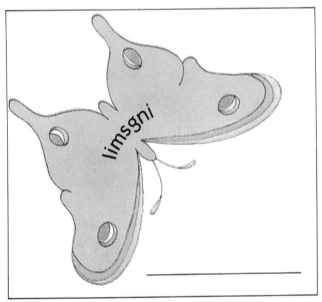

Easter Posters

To make the posters, you will need magazines and newspapers, posterboard or shelf paper, paste or glue, and felt-tip markers.

1. Your teacher will divide the class into four groups.

2. Read and follow the directions for your group.

Group 1: Find pictures of people who are praying.

Group 2: Look for pictures of people who are sharing meals and celebrating Mass together.

Group 3: Find pictures of people who are sharing God's word with others.

Group 4: Look for pictures of people of all ages who are showing love and concern for others.

3. Cut out the pictures and paste them on your group's poster. Print a title at the top of the poster.

4. Share your finished poster with the other groups. Tell your classmates about some of the ways the risen Jesus is with us now.

5. Later, display your posters in your school hallway, in the back of church, or in the parish hall.

Prayer Service for the Easter Season

Before your prayer service, gather around the Easter candle in church or around a candle in your classroom. Choose a joyful Easter song to sing. Also choose a leader and readers.

Leader: At Easter time, we are joyful. We sing happy songs. Our brother, Jesus, who died, now lives a new life. He is in heaven with God the Father, and he lives in us. Today we remember that the risen Jesus is still with us in many ways. Let us thank Jesus and give him praise.

Reader 1: Jesus, when we pray, you are close to us.

All: Thank you, Jesus. Alleluia!

Reader 2: Jesus, when we receive the Eucharist at Mass, you come to us in a very special way.

All: Thank you, Jesus. Alleluia!

Reader 3: Jesus, when we read the Bible and study about you in religion class, your words become part of us.

All: Thank you, Jesus. Alleluia!

Reader 4: Jesus, when other people love and care for us, we see your love.

All: Thank you, Jesus. Alleluia! Amen.

Our Church Honors Saints

Preaching to the Birds (oil on panel), Bonaventura Berlinghieri, 13th century, Church of San Francesco, Pescia, Italy

Saint Francis of Assisi

Many years ago in Italy, there lived a man named Francis. The town he came from was called Assisi, and so people called him Francis of Assisi.

As a young man, Francis went from town to town telling everyone about God. He told people how much God loved them. Francis loved people, too, and he helped them whenever he could. He told them how much God loved animals. Francis loved animals, too. He took such good care of the birds that they would sit on his shoulder.

Francis said that people and animals and all living things are created and loved by God. Francis called all created things his brothers and sisters.

This is part of a poem that Francis wrote to thank God for all the gifts of creation.

Song of Creation

Praise to you, O Lord,
for our brother, the sun.
He brings us the day
and gives us your light.

Praise to you, O Lord,
for our sister, the moon,
and the stars of the sky,
your gifts in the night.

Praise to you, O Lord,
for our dear sister water.
We need her to live.
She is cool, clean, and clear.

Praise to you, O Lord,
for our strong brother fire.
He warms us and cheers us
when darkness is near.

Activity

Use the clues below to fill in the crossword puzzle.

Down

1. This is a gift from God that we need to live.
2. This is the name of the town from which Francis came.
4. These twinkle in the night sky.
7. This gift gives us light at night. Francis called it sister _____.

Across

3. This gift gives us the light of day. Francis called it brother _____.
5. We need this gift when the earth is dry.
6. Francis made friends with the _____.
8. Francis thanked and praised _____ for all the gifts of God's creation.

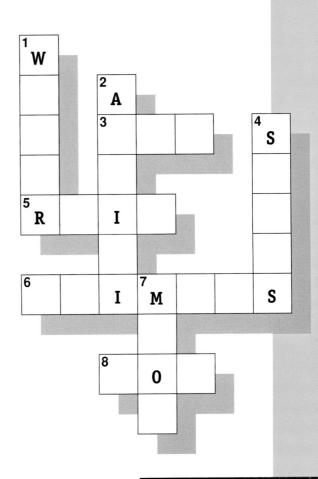

Saint Peter, Leader of the Church

The apostles had been with Jesus for three years. When Jesus healed the sick, they were there. When he told the people about God's love, they were there. When he taught the people how to pray, the apostles listened carefully.

Jesus wanted his work to go on. He wanted the good news of God's love to be shared with everyone.

Jesus had chosen his apostles with care. Soon he would go back to his Father. Now it was time to choose a leader.

One time, Jesus asked, "Who do people say that I am?"

"Some people say that you are John the Baptizer come back to life or one of the other great prophets," the apostles answered.

"Who do *you* say that I am?" Jesus continued.

Simon answered, "You are the Redeemer, God's Son."

After this, Jesus changed Simon's name to *Peter*, a name that means "rock." Then Jesus said that Peter would be the leader of the Church.

At Pentecost, Peter became the leader Jesus called him to be. He led the early Church in continuing Jesus' ministries of preaching and healing.

Based on Matthew 16:13–18 and Acts 2 and 3

Activity

Leaders are important. Good leaders need to have
talents and qualities that will help those who
follow them.

Look at the list of qualities below. Choose the
four that you think are the most important for
good leadership. Write the name of a quality
within each footstep. Tell the class why you feel
each of your choices is important.

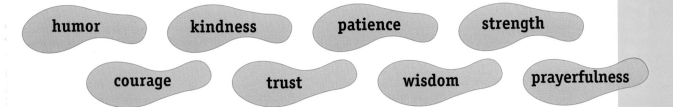

humor   kindness   patience   strength

courage   trust   wisdom   prayerfulness

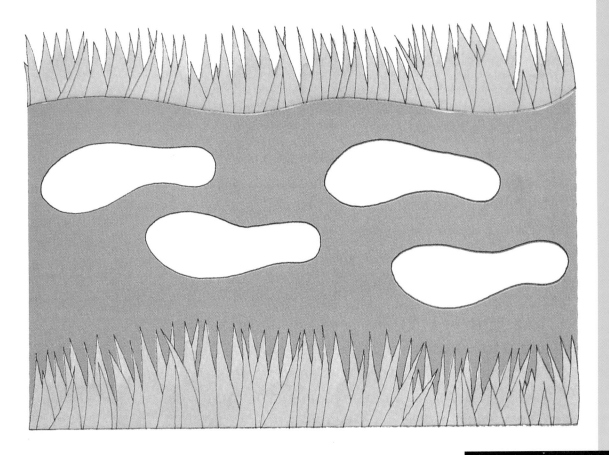

Kateri Tekakwitha

Kateri Tekakwitha was born in a Mohawk village in the woodlands of upper New York State in 1656. When she was three, a disease spread through Tekakwitha's village. Her parents died. She was left almost blind. She had to walk slowly, touching things with her hands. That is why she came to be called *Tekakwitha*, which means "She who feels her way along."

One day, a group of **Blackrobes** came to visit. Blackrobes was the name Native Americans gave to the priests who shared the gospel with them. Tekakwitha asked the priests many questions. She saw that they treated everyone with love and respect. She wanted to follow their example and become a Christian.

Tekakwitha had to wait many years for a priest to return to her village. Finally, ten years later, she was baptized and given the Christian name *Kateri*.

After her Baptism, Kateri's people made fun of her. They made it hard for her to live her faith.

Kateri heard about a Native American Christian community in Canada. It was called a "praying village." Kateri did not mind that she had to walk two hundred miles to the village. She was happy to be with people who shared her belief in Jesus.

When Kateri died, she was respected as a holy woman who cared for others. Her example led many other Native Americans to join the Catholic Church. Kateri's life teaches us that Jesus welcomes all people and that the Church is open to everyone.

Activity

The Church honors Blessed Kateri Tekakwitha on July 14th. To discover the prayer we pray on this day, unscramble the words below.

"YMA LAL LPEPOES FO VERYE RBITE DNA NOTNAI CPLOAIRM

_____

_____

OGS'D TRENGASES NI EON GOSN FO SPARIE."

_____

_____

Based on the Opening Prayer from the Memorial of Blessed Kateri Tekakwitha

Saint Teresa of Avila

Saint Teresa was born in Spain in 1515. When her mother died, Teresa's father placed her in a convent to live with the sisters. As she grew up, Teresa wanted to be a sister, too. She became a Carmelite sister at a convent near the city of Avila.

As the years went by, Sister Teresa became worried about the way she and the other sisters were living. She knew that God would want them to try harder. So Sister Teresa went from convent to convent. She showed the sisters how to pray better and reminded them to care more about one another.

Sister Teresa also wrote many books about God. Through prayer and meditation, Teresa grew very close to God. She came to understand God's ways better than many other people did. Her books became so famous that Pope Paul VI gave Teresa the title of **Doctor**, or Teacher, of the Church.

Prayer Service to Honor Saints

Teacher: There are many wonderful people in God's family. Some of them lived long ago. By learning about them, we understand better what it means for us to live as God's children. Let us ask these saints to help us to be holy as they were holy.

Reader 1: Saint Francis, you called all created things your brothers and sisters.

All: Help us to care for our world.

Reader 2: Saint Peter, Jesus chose you to be the leader of his Church.

All: Help us to be good leaders.

Reader 3: Blessed Kateri, you walked two hundred miles to be with other Christans.

All: Help us to appreciate our own Christian communities.

Reader 4: Saint Teresa, you asked the sisters to try harder to do God's will.

All: Help us to try harder.

Teacher: Let us pray.

All: Lord, you have given us many friends in heaven. Through their prayers we know that you will watch over us always and fill our hearts with your love. Amen.

Our Church Honors Mary

Feast of the Presentation of Mary

Mary is the mother of Jesus. This story is about Mary and her mother and father.

Joachim and Anne were holy people. They loved God very much and always tried to do God's will. Joachim and Anne loved each other very much, too. They wanted to have a child to care for and to love. They had been married for a long time when they finally had a little daughter, whom they called Mary. Joachim and Anne were very happy.

Mary's parents wanted her to belong to God. They wanted her to learn about God and follow the teachings of the Scriptures. When Mary was a little girl, Joachim and Anne brought her to the Temple in Jerusalem.

Each day, Mary listened to Bible stories about God and his people. She learned the prayers and songs of her people, including the **psalms**, and sang them with all her heart.

We remember the day that Joachim and Anne brought Mary to the Temple and presented her to God. We celebrate the Feast of the Presentation of Mary on November 21.

Activity

Help Mary and her parents find their way to the Temple.

Mary, Mother of Christians

After Jesus returned to the Father in heaven, the apostles, other believers, and Mary—Jesus' mother—met together often. The first Christians were like a family.

They shared everything they had. They sold the things they owned and gave the money to anyone who needed it. They broke bread together in different homes. They shared their food happily and generously, always giving praise to God. They were such a great example to others that new believers joined their group every day.

Based on the Acts of the Apostles 2:42–47

Jesus' followers loved Mary and treated her with great respect. They knew that God chose Mary to be Jesus' mother. They saw that Mary was always faithful to God and that she was filled with God's life, which we call **grace**.

When he was dying on the cross, Jesus gave Mary to us as our mother. Jesus knew that we would need Mary's example to follow him and to build his Church.

We honor Mary as the mother of Christians. Mary shows her love and care for us by bringing our prayers and worries to Jesus.

Madonna and Child seated in a landscape (oil), Jan Sanders Van Hemessen, 16th century, Rafael Valls Gallery, London, England

Activity

Solve the problems below. Find the letter that matches each correct answer. Copy the letters on the lines. Then read Mary's prayer (based on Luke 1:49).

8=A	13=S	14=N	15=G	16=D
17=E	18=M	19=H	20=R	21=O
23=Y	24=I	25=F	26=T	27=L

(9+6) (17+4) (9+7)   (27-8) (7+1) (9+4)

_____   _____

(8+8) (30-9) (9+5) (9+8)   (8+7) (37-17) (6+11) (26-18) (9+17)

_____   _____

(8+18) (7+12) (19+5) (8+6) (17-2) (29-16)

_____

(19+6) (16+5) (8+12)   (27-9) (6+11)

_____   _____.

(8+7) (14+7) (21-5) ' (7+6)   (23-9) (26-18) (6+12) (21-4)

_____   _____

(31-7) (5+8)   (15+4) (12+9) (19+8) (19+4)

_____   _____

Our Lady of Fatima, artist unknown

Our Lady of Fatima

On May 13, 1917, three children named Lucia, Jacinta, and Francisco were tending sheep in the fields near the small town of Fatima, Portugal. Suddenly they saw a lady dressed in shining white clothes. The lady told the children she was from heaven and they should not be afraid. She said that if they returned to the field each month, she would tell them who she was.

Every month, for six months, the children waited for the lady. They called her "Our Lady." She asked the children to pray the Rosary for peace in the world. She reminded them that God wanted everyone to turn away from sin and to live good lives.

Some people who heard about Our Lady's visits did not believe it. Others wanted to see if it were true. They went to the field and waited, but only the children could see her. Lucia asked Our Lady to show them a sign so that everyone would believe in her.

On Our Lady's last visit to Fatima, 100,000 people waited and prayed with the children. She said that she was Our Lady of the Rosary. She asked them to build a church for her. People reported that she then gave everyone the sign she had promised. They said that for ten minutes the sun changed colors and seemed to dance and spin in the sky and that Our Lady then appeared to the children once again—with Saint Joseph and Jesus beside her!

The next year, a church was built in honor of Our Lady of Fatima. Millions of people visit this holy place every year to pray and to remember the visits of Mary. We can remember Our Lady of Fatima each time we pray the Rosary. The message of Fatima is that Mary is always watching over us, guiding us to Jesus.

Activity

Mary asked Lucia, Jacinta, and Francisco to pray for peace. What do you think Mary wants us to pray for today? Write your ideas here.

_____

_____

_____

_____

Our Church Celebrates Holy Days

Communion of Saints (fresco), Andrea da Firenze, 14th century, Spanish Chapel, Santa Maria Novella, Florence, Italy

Feast of All Saints

Each year the Church celebrates the union of the members of God's family. We celebrate this day on November 1, the Feast of All Saints.

On this day we celebrate what it means to belong to God's family. We come together at Mass to remember the great saints like Mary and Joseph and Francis and many, many more. We think of all the good people we have known who have died and gone to be with God in heaven. And we think about what it means to live as a member of God's family on earth today.

On the Feast of All Saints we pray this prayer.

God, our Father,
You are all powerful and always alive.
Today we are happy as we remember
    all the holy men, women, and children
    of every time and place.
May their care for us help us to be
    your holy sons and daughters, too,
    so that one day we will celebrate with you
    and with them in the happiness of heaven.
Amen.   Based on the Opening Prayer
                               from the Feast of All Saints

Activity

Match the name of each person with the words
that tell something about that person.

1. Mary   _____ someone living today who is
                                   trying to be a saint

2. Peter   _____ one of the twelve apostles

3. Francis   _____ the mother of Jesus

4. Joseph   _____ a member of the Holy Family

5. _____   _____ someone who lived long ago
    (Fill in your name.)   who loved all God's creation

Holy Trinity

Jesus asked his apostles to go to a mountain in Galilee. When they saw the risen Jesus, they began to worship him. Jesus said, "All the power in heaven and on earth has been given to me. Go to the people of every nation and make them my disciples. Baptize them in the name of the Father, the Son, and the Holy Spirit. Teach them to do everything that I have commanded you. Remember, I am with you always, even until the end of the world."

Based on Matthew 28:16–20

The Church honors the Holy **Trinity** on the Sunday after Pentecost Sunday. We believe that there are three Persons in the one God: God the Father, God the Son, and God the Holy Spirit. The three Persons in God each have an important place in our lives as Catholics. Each time we make the Sign of the Cross, we say that we believe in the Holy Trinity. We believe that God the Father created us. We believe that God the Son, Jesus, saved us from sin and death and shares his new life with us. We believe that God the Holy Spirit helps and guides us as we grow in holiness.

Activity

We can honor the Holy Trinity when we pray. Complete the Glory Be by filling in the missing words. Then pray it aloud with your class.

Glory be to the _____ ,

and to the _____ ,

and to the _____ .

As it was in the _____ ,

is _____ , and ever shall be,

_____ without _____ . Amen.

Christ the King

On the last Sunday of the Church year, just before Advent begins, we celebrate the Feast of Christ the King. We read in the Gospels that many people expected that God would send a great ruler to be their king. Jesus explained that he was not the kind of king they expected. He also told them that his kingdom would be much better than they imagined.

Jesus' kingdom is not a country or land. Jesus spoke about a kingdom in which there would be **justice** for everyone. All people would be treated with respect and care. He said that it would be a kingdom of peace. People would be welcomed regardless of who they are, and everyone would learn to be forgiving.

Christ Enthroned (icon, enamel on gold), 12th century, Russia

The Scripture readings that we sometimes hear on the Feast of Christ the King remind us that Jesus leads his followers as a shepherd leads his sheep. He loves them and cares for them. He guides them gently. The Scripture readings also remind us that Jesus is a powerful and loving king! Jesus taught that by acting in the ways that he taught us, we can help show others the way to the kingdom.

The word **Christ** means "the anointed one." In the time of Jesus, kings were anointed or blessed with oil. It was a sign that they had been called to special work. Jesus, God's Anointed One, was called by God to save us from sin and death. Jesus saves us by his life, death, and resurrection.

Activity

Think about how you can help make your family, school, and neighborhood more like the kingdom that Jesus taught about. Then complete the sentences below.

I will be a peacemaker. I will _____

_____

_____

_____.

I will show my love for Jesus by loving others. I will

_____

_____

_____.

I will treat people fairly. I will _____

_____

_____

_____.

In the Spirit of Jesus

Mother Teresa

Many young girls in Yugoslavia wanted to be sisters. Agnes Gonxha Bojaxhiu was one of them. She wanted to serve God with her whole heart and soul. In 1928, when Agnes was eighteen, she joined a convent in India. The name that was given to her was Sister Teresa.

Sister Teresa was sent to teach at St. Mary's High School in Calcutta, a very large city in India. Each day when she prayed, Sister Teresa asked for help to know what God wanted her to do. "One day," she says, "I heard the call to give up all and to follow God into the slums to serve among the poorest of the poor."

In 1948 she opened a school in the slums. At the same time, she was learning how to care for the many sick people of Calcutta. Most of them were too poor to go to a hospital. Every day, hundreds of poor people would die in the streets, with no one to help them.

Soon other young women came to help Teresa, who was now called Mother Teresa. They called their new group the Missionaries of Charity. Today, there are more than 3,000 of these sisters, in nearly sixty countries throughout the world, who help the poorest of the poor.

Activity

There are ten words hidden in the puzzle. The words tell what Mother Teresa and the women in her community share with people. Some words read across and others read down. Find each word and circle it.

A	C	L	O	T	H	I	N	G	E	H	S
H	T	E	I	S	Y	D	G	O	M	P	H
O	W	R	S	D	F	O	O	D	Y	X	E
P	E	A	C	E	L	U	W	A	C	O	L
E	M	R	U	V	G	M	E	B	E	F	T
Y	J	D	A	M	E	D	I	C	I	N	E
L	O	V	E	F	N	Z	O	W	Y	M	R
B	Y	X	F	U	D	C	A	R	E	P	O

Catholic Relief Services

Shanna was watching the news on television with her family. "We now turn to the problems in Bosnia," said the announcer. "Thousands of people have left their homes to escape from the war."

Shanna watched the long lines of people walking slowly along dirt roads. They carried their belongings in baskets and cardboard boxes. "Oh, those poor families," said Shanna. "Where can they go?"

The television showed a crowded camp. The announcer said, "Catholic Relief Services has set up centers to give food, water, and shelter to the villagers. When the war is over, the workers will stay in Bosnia to rebuild the villages. If you would like to help, copy the address that appears on your screen."

"Can *we* help the villagers?" asked Shanna.

"Yes, Shanna," said her mother. "We will send a contribution tomorrow. Tonight, when we say our prayers, we will ask God to help them."

Catholic Relief Services was begun by the National Conference of Catholic Bishops of the United States in 1943. The bishops wanted to help people living overseas who had lost their homes during the Second World War.

Today, Catholic Relief Services works in over seventy-five countries. CRS helps in many ways. They find homes for orphans. They have built silos to help people in Haiti store grain. They have dug water wells in India. And they teach farmers in Africa to grow crops.

Catholic Relief Services works in the spirit of Jesus to care for poor, suffering, and forgotten people all over the world. Catholic Relief Services helps us to remember that all people are part of one big family—the family of God.

Activity

The scrambled words tell us the command that the workers of Catholic Relief Services live every day. Unscramble the words and write them on the lines below.

OYU
SMTU
VEOL
OURY
BRINGEHO
SA
LYORFSUE

_____ _____

_____ _____

_____ _____

_____ .

OUR CATHOLIC HERITAGE

We can know, live, and celebrate our faith. Catholics do this in special ways.

 The Bible

The Bible is divided into two parts: the Old Testament and the New Testament. Each part contains many books. There are 46 books in the Old Testament. These books tell us about God's people before Jesus was born.

There are 27 books in the New Testament. They tell us about the life of Jesus, the early Christians, and the beginnings of the Church.

Each book of the Bible has its own name. Each book is divided into chapters, which are numbered. And each chapter is divided into verses. The verses are also numbered.

Finding a story in the Bible is really very easy. Look, for example, at the story of John the Baptizer on pages 244 and 245 in your book. If you wanted to find this story in the Bible, you would need to look in the New Testament and find Luke 7:18–23. In other words, you would find the book called The Gospel According to Luke, chapter 7, verses 18 through 23.

Luke	7:	18–23
book of the Bible	chapter number	verse numbers

The Holy Land

GALILEE

Great Sea
(Mediterranean Sea)

Sea of
Galilee

Cana ●
Nazareth ●

SAMARIA

River Jordan

North

Emmaus ●

Jerusalem ●

Jericho ●

Bethlehem ●

Dead
Sea

JUDEA

The Trinity

We Believe in God

There is only one God. We know God as three distinct Persons: God the Father, God the Son, and God the Holy Spirit. We believe that there is one God in three Persons, whom we call the **Blessed Trinity**.

God is all-good, all-holy, and all-knowing. God is always just and merciful.

God the Father speaks to us in many ways. We know the Father especially through Jesus, the Scriptures, and the Church.

God created all things out of love. We share the gift of God's life and love. Catholics call this sharing in God's life **grace**. With grace, we help God care for the world.

We Believe in Jesus

Jesus, God's own Son, is the second Person of the Blessed Trinity. Jesus is both God and man. Jesus is human like us in all things but sin.

God sent Jesus to us to show us how to live. Jesus taught us about God's love. Jesus gave his life for us. Jesus died on the cross and rose from the dead. Jesus is our **Savior**. He saves us from sin and brings us new life. Jesus sent the Holy Spirit to help us live our new life.

We Believe in the Holy Spirit

The Holy Spirit is the third Person of the Blessed Trinity. The Holy Spirit is our helper and guide. The Spirit helps us live as followers of Jesus.

The Holy Spirit came on **Pentecost**. The Holy Spirit gave the disciples the courage to share Jesus' good news. The Holy Spirit is with the Church today, helping us to be a sign of Jesus. We receive the Holy Spirit at Baptism.

ABOUT The Catholic Church

Catholics are followers of Jesus who spread God's word, worship God, celebrate the sacraments, and serve those in need.

The Church has four marks, or signs: that it is one, holy, catholic, and apostolic.

We are one because we are united. Our belief in Jesus unites us.

We are holy because we love God and try to live the Gospel by caring for others.

We are catholic because the Church welcomes people of all kinds, as Jesus does.

We are apostolic because our teachings are true to the teachings of Jesus and his apostles.

The **pope** is the leader of the Catholic Church. We call the pope our Holy Father.

ABOUT Mary and the Saints

Mary is the mother of Jesus. From the first moment of life, Mary was filled with grace. Mary is our mother, too. Mary loves and cares for us.

Mary is our greatest **saint**. Saints are special people who showed us how to follow Jesus. We honor the saints and ask them to pray for us.

Pieta (ivory), 15th century, Spain

ABOUT Life Everlasting

Jesus teaches us that if we follow his example we will be happy forever in **heaven**. Heaven is unending happiness with God and all who love God. If we show love for God, ourselves, and others, we will be happy together in heaven.

Even today, we are part of the **communion of saints**. The communion of saints is the community of all those, living and dead, who believe in Jesus Christ.

How Catholics Worship

Catholics have a sacred history of **worship**. Worship is giving honor and praise to God. Through the sacraments and prayer, we praise, thank, and adore God, and ask God's help.

ABOUT The Sacraments

The **sacraments** are sacred signs that celebrate God's love for us and Jesus' presence in our lives. There are seven sacraments. Through the sacraments, we are united with Jesus.

Each sacrament has special words and actions. The words and actions are signs that God is present.

The Sacraments of Initiation We become full members of the Church through the three sacraments of initiation. The sacraments of initiation are Baptism, Confirmation, and Eucharist.

Baptism is a sacrament of welcome into the Church community. We receive the Holy Spirit and begin to share Jesus' new life.

In the celebration the priest or deacon pours water over the head of the person being baptized and prays, "I baptize you in the name of the Father, and of the Son, and of the Holy Spirit."

from the *Rite of Baptism*

Confirmation strengthens the new life we received at Baptism and helps us tell everyone the good news about Jesus.

In the celebration the bishop or priest lays his hand on the head of the one to be confirmed and anoints the forehead with holy oil as he prays, "Be sealed with the Gift of the Holy Spirit."

from the *Rite of Confirmation*

Eucharist celebrates the real presence of Jesus.

In the celebration the priest says the words of consecration over the bread and wine, which become the body and blood of Christ.

The Sacraments of Healing The sacraments of healing—Reconciliation and the Anointing of the Sick—celebrate God's forgiveness and healing.

Reconciliation celebrates God's healing and forgiveness of our sins.

In the celebration the priest prays the prayer of absolution, ending with the words, "I absolve you from your sins in the name of the Father, and of the Son, and of the Holy Spirit."

from the *Rite of Penance*

The Anointing of the Sick brings God's help and peace to sick people.

In the celebration the priest anoints the person with the oil of the sick as he prays, "Through this holy anointing may the Lord in his love and mercy help you with the grace of the Holy Spirit."

from the *Rite of Anointing*

The Sacraments of Commitment In the sacraments of commitment, the Church celebrates two special ways that people serve others by sharing their gifts. The sacraments of commitment are Matrimony and Holy Orders.

Matrimony celebrates the lifelong love of a man and a woman.

In the celebration the bride and groom make special promises to each other.

In **Holy Orders** bishops, priests, and deacons are ordained to serve the Church in a special way.

In the celebration the bishop lays his hands on the head of the person to be ordained. Afterward, he prays a special prayer of blessing.

ABOUT The Mass

Introductory Rites

At Mass, we come together to pray and worship as the family of Jesus.

Entrance Procession and Gathering Song

As the priest and other ministers enter in procession, we stand and sing a gathering song.

Greeting

We make the Sign of the Cross. The priest welcomes us by saying, "The Lord be with you." We answer, "And also with you."

Penitential Rite

As a community, we admit that we have sinned and we thank God for the gift of forgiveness. We pray the opening prayer.

Gloria

We sing or say this hymn of praise to God.

Liturgy of the Word

First Reading

The lector reads a story about God's love for us, usually from the Old Testament.

Responsorial Psalm

The song leader sings a psalm from the Bible. We join in singing a response.

Second Reading

The lector reads from the New Testament, usually from one of the letters.

Gospel Acclamation

Before the Gospel is proclaimed by the priest or deacon, we sing, "Alleluia" or another acclamation.

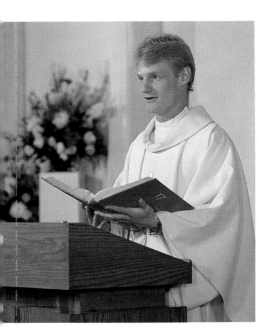

Gospel

In honor of Jesus, who speaks to us in the Gospel reading, we stand as it is proclaimed.

Homily

The priest or deacon explains the readings, especially the Gospel, in a special talk called the homily.

Profession of Faith

We stand to declare our beliefs. We recite the Nicene Creed.

General Intercessions

We pray for the pope and the bishops, for our country, and for all God's people.

Liturgy of the Eucharist

Preparation of the Altar and the Gifts

As the table is prepared, we bring gifts of bread and wine to the altar. The priest offers our gifts to God.

Eucharistic Prayer

In this prayer of praise and thanksgiving, the priest addresses God our Creator in our name. Together we sing a song of praise for God's many blessings, especially Jesus.

We sing or say,

"Holy, holy, holy Lord, God of power and might. Heaven and earth are full of your glory. Hosanna in the highest. Blessed is he who comes in the name of the Lord. Hosanna in the highest."

The priest calls upon the Holy Spirit and asks that the bread and wine become Jesus' body and blood. The priest consecrates the bread and wine. We proclaim the mystery of faith. We sing or say these or other words,

"Christ has died,
Christ is risen,
Christ will come again."

As the Eucharistic Prayer ends, we say, "Amen."

Communion Rite

The Lord's Prayer

We pray together the prayer that Jesus taught us—The Lord's Prayer.

Sign of Peace

We offer each other a sign of peace to show that we are all brothers and sisters in Jesus.

Breaking of the Bread

While the priest breaks the bread, we sing or say, "Lamb of God, you take away the sins of the world: have mercy on us.

Lamb of God, you take away the sins of the world: have mercy on us.

Lamb of God, you take away the sins of the world: grant us peace."

Communion

Jesus invites us to share his body and blood in the Eucharist.

Concluding Rite

Blessing

The priest blesses us in the name of God the Father, God the Son, and God the Holy Spirit. We answer, "Amen."

Dismissal

The priest tells us to go in peace to love and serve God and others. We sing a song of thanks and praise.

ABOUT Reconciliation

In the sacrament of Penance, or Reconciliation, I celebrate God's forgiveness.

Preparation I think about my words and actions in my examination of conscience. I feel sorrow for my sins.

Rite of Reconciliation of Individuals

Priest's Welcome The priest welcomes me in the name of Jesus and the Church.

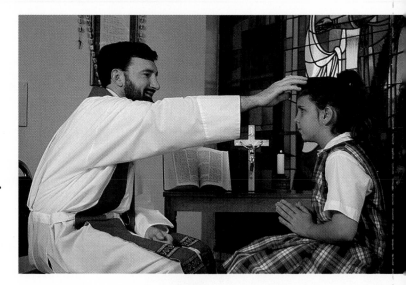

Reading from Scripture The priest may read a part of the Bible with me.

Confession I tell the priest my sins. The priest suggests ways that I might love God more. He asks me to say a prayer or do a kind act, called an act of penance, to show that I am sorry.

Prayer of Sorrow The priest asks me to tell God I am sorry for my sins. I say aloud a prayer of sorrow, called an act of contrition.

Absolution Acting in the name of the Church, the priest extends his hands over me and asks God to forgive me. The priest gives me absolution in the name of the Father, Son, and Holy Spirit.

Prayer of Praise and Dismissal With the priest, I praise God. The priest tells me to go in peace. I answer, "Amen."

Celebrating Reconciliation in Community

Introductory Rites We sing an opening song. The priest invites us to pray for God's forgiveness.

The Word of God We listen to readings from the Bible. The priest gives a homily.

Examination of Conscience The priest helps us to examine our conscience. We sing or say The Lord's Prayer.

Rite of Reconciliation Together we pray a prayer of sorrow. Then, one by one, we go to confession and receive absolution.

Proclamation of Praise for God's Mercy We praise and thank God for his mercy.

Concluding Rites The priest blesses us. We sing a song of praise and thanksgiving.

How Catholics Live

The teachings of Jesus and the Church show us how Catholics live happy and loving lives.

 The Beatitudes

The Beatitudes are Jesus' teachings on how to find everlasting happiness. They teach us to love God and others. Christians believe that they are promised a place in the kingdom of heaven if they live the Beatitudes.

The Beatitudes	How We Live the Beatitudes
Happy are the poor in spirit. The reign of God is theirs.	We are poor in spirit when we know that we need God more than anything else in life.
Happy are the sorrowing. They will be comforted.	We obey God and trust in his goodness. We try to help those who are hurting. We know that God is with them.
Happy are the gentle. They will receive all that God has promised.	We are kind and loving. We use the gifts that God has given us to help others.
Happy are those who hunger and thirst for justice. They will be satisfied.	We work to lead others to God's kingdom. We share the things we have with those in need.
Happy are those who show mercy to others. They will receive mercy.	We forgive anyone who has hurt us. We accept others and are patient with them.
Happy are the single-hearted. They will see God.	We show our love for God by loving our neighbor.
Happy are the peacemakers. They will be called children of God.	We try to bring God's peace to the world. We help people make up after a fight.
Happy are those who are treated unfairly for doing what is right. The reign of God is theirs.	We carry on Jesus' work in the world. We stand up for what is right, even though it is not always easy.

The Commandments

Jesus said it is important to obey the Ten Commandments. The commandments help us live as children of God.

The Ten Commandments	The Commandments Help Us to Live
1. I, the Lord, am your God. You shall not have other gods besides me.	We believe in and love God more than anyone or anything else in life. We remember God's gifts to us. We talk to and listen to God in prayer.
2. You shall not take the name of the Lord, your God, in vain.	We use the names of God, Jesus, and all holy persons, places, and things with respect and love. We never say God's or Jesus' name in anger.
3. Remember to keep holy the Sabbath day.	We worship God by celebrating the Eucharist together on Sunday. We relax and do special things on Sunday in honor of God.
4. Honor your father and mother.	We love, respect, and obey our parents and all adults who care for us.
5. You shall not kill.	We show respect for God's gift of life by caring for all human life. We never fight or hurt others.
6. You shall not commit adultery.	We respect our bodies and the bodies of others. We use our sexuality according to God's plan.
7. You shall not steal.	We never take things that belong to someone else. We are careful with other people's things. We do not cheat.
8. You shall not bear false witness against your neighbor.	We are truthful and honest. We never tell lies or hurt others by what we say.
9. You shall not covet your neighbor's wife.	We respect the promises that married people have made to each other.
10. You shall not covet anything that belongs to your neighbor.	We are satisfied with what we have. We are not jealous or greedy.

The Great Commandment

"Love God with all your heart, all your thoughts, and all your strength, and love your neighbor as yourself" (based on Mark 12:28–31).

Jesus summed up the Ten Commandments in the **Great Commandment**, which teaches us that God's laws are based on love of God and love of neighbor.

The New Commandment

"This is my commandment: love one another as I love you" (John 15:12).

Jesus' love is the perfect example of how to live. We must love as Jesus loved. Our love for one another is a sign of Jesus' love.

ABOUT Sin and Grace

Sin keeps us from living as Jesus' followers. Sin is a free choice to turn away from God's love. We sin by doing something we know is wrong, or we may sin by not doing what we know is right. By sharing in the gift of God's life and love, we have the grace to live as children of God, to be freed from our sins, and to be forgiven.

The Holy Spirit helps us turn away from sin and live as followers of Jesus. The Holy Spirit helps us make good choices. The Holy Spirit helps us know if something is right or wrong. We can pray to the Holy Spirit when we have a difficult choice to make.

ABOUT Vocations

When we were baptized, we began our new life as Christians. Our parents and godparents wanted to share with us their Catholic faith. As we grow older, we will live more and more as Jesus taught us. We will be invited by God to choose many ways of helping others. God's call to each of us to help others in a special way is called our **vocation**.

Many Ways of Helping

Most Catholics are called by God to help others as members of their parish church. Some of the ways they help at Mass are by reading the Scriptures, leading music, or serving the Eucharist. Other ways to help include teaching others about God's love for them and working to help people who are poor.

Some vocations are celebrated as sacraments in the Church. **Bishops** and priests are called to lead the Catholic community in celebrating the sacraments and in teaching God's word. **Deacons** are also called to serve as leaders in the Church. Deacons often preach homilies, celebrate the sacraments of Baptism and Matrimony, and help direct the work of the parish among the poor.

Religious Sisters and Brothers, who dedicate their lives to serving others through the work of the Church, live in communities among other religious Sisters and Brothers. They make promises to God and to their communities that they will live simply and do the work that their communities help lead them to do.

Many other men and women, who do not belong to religious communities, also commit their lives to serving others full time through the work of the Church. These men and women serve as religious educators, musicians, Catholic school teachers, hospital workers, and lay missionaries. They all help the Catholic community to live as Jesus taught us to live.

ABOUT Missionaries

The Church reaches out to people who need to hear the good news of Jesus and invites them to join the Catholic Christian community. **Missionaries** are men and women, religious Brothers and Sisters, and priests who work in places where the Church needs to grow. Some of those places are here in our country. Others are in countries throughout the world. Missionaries often work among the poor and others who have needs that the Church can help meet. Some missionaries teach people how to grow crops for food. Others teach better health care methods or ways to organize schools.

Missionaries often build Catholic communities among the people with whom they work. They welcome the people into the Church. They celebrate Mass and the sacraments with their new communities. They teach others how to be leaders in the Church so that these communities can grow.

HOW CATHOLICS PRAY

Through prayer, Catholics express their faith and show their love for God and others. The Church is united through the celebration of the sacraments and the prayers of all of its members.

ABOUT Kinds of Prayer

Prayer is listening and talking to God. We can pray for the needs of others. We can make our whole life a prayer. We can greet God in the morning with prayer. We can pray before meals. We can thank God for our day before we go to sleep. God always hears our prayers.

Quiet Prayer is a way of praying without words. When we pray in silence, God speaks to us in our heart. We can pray quietly by remembering a Bible story or by using our imagination to think of God, Jesus, the Holy Spirit, or Mary. As we pray, we can think about our life with God.

The **Rosary** is a prayer honoring Mary. When we pray the Rosary, we repeat the Hail Mary over and over. We praise Mary and remember some of the most important times in the lives of Jesus and Mary. Praying the Rosary helps us grow closer to Mary and to her son, Jesus.

13 Jesus Is Taken Down from the Cross

Thank you, Jesus, for giving
your life for us.

14

2 Jesus Accepts the Cross

Help me, Jesus, to always
do the right thing.

13

Jesus Is Alive

Thank you, Jesus,
for being with us always.

16

STATIONS OF THE CROSS

3 **Jesus Falls the First Time**

Help me, Jesus, to do my best.

4

12 **Jesus Dies**

Thank you, Jesus,
for loving us so much.

13

1 **Jesus Is Condemned to Death**

Help me, Jesus, when I am
all alone.

2

14 **Jesus Is Buried**

Thank you, Jesus,
for new life.

15

9 Jesus Falls the Third Time

Help me, Jesus, to help others
when they are sad.

10

6 Veronica Wipes the Face of Jesus

Help me, Jesus, to share
with others.

7

11 Jesus Is Nailed to the Cross

Help me, Jesus,
when I am hurt.

12

4 Jesus Meets His Mother

Help me, Jesus, to obey
my parents and teachers.

5

7 **Jesus Falls the Second Time**

Help me, Jesus, to always
keep trying.

8

8 **Jesus Meets the Women**

Help me, Jesus, to love
all people.

9

5 **Simon Takes the Cross**

Help me, Jesus, to care
for others.

6

10 **Jesus Is Stripped of His Clothes**

Help me, Jesus, when I
am afraid.

11

ABOUT The Lord's Prayer

Jesus taught his friends The Lord's Prayer. In this special prayer, we honor God. We pray that what God wants will be done. We ask God for the things that we need.

Our Father, who art in heaven, hallowed be thy name.
God is our Father. We pray that everyone will remember how good God is.

Thy kingdom come.
Jesus told us about God's kingdom. We pray that everyone will live as Jesus taught us to live.

Thy will be done on earth as it is in heaven.
We pray that everyone will obey God's laws.

Praying with sign-language gestures

Give us this day our daily bread.

We know that God cares for us. We pray for our needs and the needs of the poor.

And forgive us our trespasses as we forgive those who trespass against us.

We ask God to forgive us for the wrong things we have done.

And lead us not into temptation.

We ask God to help us always to choose what is right.

But deliver us from evil.

We pray that God will protect us from things that may harm us.

Amen.

Our "Amen" says that this is our prayer, too.

anointing

putting blessed oil on a person's body as a sign of love, respect, or honor *(page 135)*

Anointing of the Sick

the sacrament of comfort and strength, of forgiveness, healing, and peace *(pages 135, 335)*

Apostles' Creed

a summary of what Catholics and many other Christians believe *(page 95)*

apostolic

founded on and faithful to the teachings of Jesus and his apostles *(page 43)*

Ash Wednesday

the first day of the season of Lent *(page 282)*

Baptism

a sacrament of welcome into the Church community in which we receive the Holy Spirit and begin to share Jesus' new life *(page 333)*

baptismal font

a container for water that is used in Baptism *(page 129)*

baptismal pool

a larger baptismal font in which a person can kneel, stand, or be immersed *(page 129)*

bishop

pastoral leader of a diocese *(pages 215, 346)*

Blackrobes

a name for priests who shared the gospel with Native Americans *(page 306)*

Blessed Trinity

one God in three Persons *(page 330)*

Calvary

the hill where Jesus was crucified *(page 280)*

catholic

open to and accepting of people everywhere *(page 35)*

Catholic Church

the Christian community which celebrates the seven sacraments and recognizes the pope and bishops as its leaders *(page 17)*

Catholics

followers of Jesus who spread God's word, worship God, celebrate the sacraments, and serve those in need *(page 331)*

Christ

the anointed one *(page 321)*

Glossary

Christians

the worldwide community of people who believe that Jesus is the Son of God *(page 13)*

commandments

laws given to us by God to help us live good lives *(page 165)*

communion of saints

the community of all those, living and dead, who believe in Jesus Christ *(page 332)*

Confirmation

a sacrament of welcome which strengthens the new life we received at Baptism and helps us tell everyone the good news about Jesus *(page 334)*

corporal

affecting our bodies and the needs of our bodies *(page 185)*

crux gemmata

a cross decorated with precious stones or jewels *(page 287)*

deacon

a person ordained to help the priest in serving the parish community in many different ways *(pages 215, 346)*

diocese

a community of many parishes that are located near one another *(page 215)*

Doctor

Teacher of the Church *(page 308)*

Easter Vigil

the night before Easter, when the Church celebrates new life in Christ and the resurrection of Jesus, the Light of the World *(page 127)*

epistles

the letters, written mostly by Paul, that became part of the New Testament in the Bible *(page 229)*

Eucharist

a sacrament of welcome that celebrates the real presence of Jesus in the consecrated bread and wine we share *(page 334)*

faith

the belief that Jesus loves us and our response to God's call *(page 47)*

faithful

someone who is always with us and always caring; someone who is to be trusted and depended upon *(page 65)*

gospel

the good news of Jesus' love for all people *(page 43)*

grace

sharing in the gift of God's life and love *(pages 312, 330)*

Great Commandment

the commandment to love God and others and which teaches us that God's laws are based on love of God and love of neighbor *(page 344)*

healing

the actions, words, and prayers that help people who are hurting to become well, to feel better, or to be forgiven *(page 133)*

heaven

unending happiness with God and all who love God *(page 332)*

holy

being close to God, loving God and others, and doing his work in the world *(page 23)*

Holy Orders

the sacrament in which bishops, priests, and deacons are ordained to special service in the Church *(pages 147, 335)*

Holy Week

the week from Palm Sunday to Easter in which we remember the important events in the last week of Jesus' life on earth *(page 292)*

immersion

baptizing a new Christian by placing his or her whole body under water *(page 129)*

initiation

how new members learn more about and are welcomed into a group *(page 123)*

Jesse Tree

Jesus' family tree that has symbols of Jesus' ancestors on it *(page 264)*

justice

treating everyone fairly and with respect *(pages 243, 320)*

lector

a minister of the word who proclaims God's word at Mass *(page 227)*

liturgy

the official public prayers of the Church *(page 117)*

Liturgy of the Hours

the official prayers of the Church that some Christians pray together every morning and every evening *(page 117)*

marks of the Church

signs of the Church that show it is one, holy, catholic, and apostolic *(page 43)*

Matrimony

the sacrament that celebrates the lifelong and life-giving love between a man and a woman, who promise to love each other as husband and wife *(pages 149, 335)*

Glossary

mercy

loving care or compassion *(page 185)*

ministry

the ways we serve God and all people according to God's special call *(page 213)*

ministry of community building

ways in which we help the Church to grow in unity *(page 213)*

ministry of service

reaching out to people in need and working to change situations and attitudes that cause people's pain and suffering *(page 245)*

ministry of the word

serving others by sharing God's word with them *(page 223)*

ministry of worship

helping people to pray and take part in community worship *(page 235)*

mission

the work God calls us to do *(page 282)*

missionaries

people who are sent out to spread the gospel throughout the world *(pages 49, 347)*

myrrh

a special perfume put on a person's body when he or she has died *(page 276)*

parables

brief stories that helped people understand what Jesus taught *(page 183)*

parish

a special community where followers of Jesus come together to pray and share stories of our faith *(page 17)*

pastor

a priest who leads a parish community *(page 215)*

Pentecost

the birthday of the Church; the day on which Jesus' first disciples received the gift of the Holy Spirit *(pages 85, 331)*

Pharisees

very religious Jews who based their entire lives on living according to God's laws *(page 163)*

pope

bishop of Rome and leader of the Catholic Church all over the world *(pages 215, 331)*

praise

a way to show or tell God how wonderful he is and how grateful we are to him *(page 233)*

prayer

listening and talking to God through our words, our songs, and our gestures *(pages 113, 348)*

prophet

someone called by God to speak in his name *(pages 225, 268)*

psalms

songs of prayer from the Old Testament *(pages 115, 311)*

Reconciliation

sacrament of healing in which we celebrate God's healing and forgiveness of our sins *(page 334)*

respect

to act with care toward someone or something *(page 39)*

resurrection

Jesus' rising from death to new life *(page 75)*

reverence

an attitude of respect, care, and honor *(page 175)*

ritual

the words, actions, and gestures that we use to remember or celebrate something very meaningful *(page 290)*

Rosary

a prayer honoring Mary that recalls some of the most important times in the lives of Jesus and Mary *(page 348)*

Sabbath

a day for rest and prayer *(page 163)*

sacraments

special celebrations of the Church that show Jesus' love for us and are signs of his presence with us now *(pages 113, 333)*

saints

holy men and women who are honored by the Church because they showed in extraordinary ways that they loved God and others unselfishly *(pages 27, 332)*

Savior

a name for Jesus, who saves us from sin and brings us new life *(page 330)*

scribes

well-educated Jews who studied God's law and explained it to people *(page 165)*

Glossary

Scriptures

the written word of God *(page 15)*

sin

anything we do or say that we know is wrong and may hurt others and our relationship with God *(pages 137, 282, 344)*

spiritual

affecting the mind, heart, or spirit *(page 195)*

Stations of the Cross

a devotional prayer that helps us remember how much Jesus loves us and how he died for us *(page 280)*

synagogue

a special place where Jewish people pray and study God's word *(page 115)*

tomb

a place where a person's dead body is laid to rest *(page 294)*

Triduum

the three holiest days of the Church year; from Holy Thursday evening through Easter Sunday evening *(page 290)*

Trinity

the one God whom we know as three distinct Persons: God the Father, God the Son, and God the Holy Spirit *(pages 67, 319)*

trust

to have faith in God's love for us and to believe that he is always with us *(page 63)*

twelve apostles

those chosen by Jesus to teach and lead his friends and followers *(page 15)*

vocation

God's call to develop and use our own unique gifts for our own good and the good of others *(pages 145, 345)*

witness

one who shares what he or she knows about Jesus and lives in the ways that Jesus wants us to live *(page 49)*

worship

to give honor and praise to God, especially as a community *(pages 235, 333)*

Index

Index